I DARED TO CALL HIM

Father

Bilquis Sheikh with Richard H. Schneider

I DARED TO CALL HIM
CALL HIM
Father

published by

√ chosen books

of The Zondervan Corporation/Grand Rapids, Michigan 49506

Library of Congress Cataloging in Publication Data

Sheikh, Bilquis.
    I dared to call him Father.
  1. Sheikh, Bilquis. 2. Converts from Islam—Biography. I. Schneider, Richard, 1922–
I. Title.
BV2626.4.S53A33   248'.246'0924 [B]   77–15603

ISBN 0-310-60031-6

Chosen Books is a division of The Zondervan Corporation, Grand Rapids, Michigan 49506. Editorial offices for Chosen Books are in Lincoln, Virginia 22078.

To my grandson Mahmud
my little prayer partner
who has been a source of
joy and comfort to me
through many lonely hours.

Contents

Foreword   9
1. A Frightening Presence   15
2. The Strange Book   26
3. The Dreams   33
4. The Encounter   39
5. The Crossroads   52
6. Learning to Find His Presence   60
7. The Baptism of Fire and Water   70
8. Was There Protection?   81
9. The Boycott   94
10. Learning to Live in the Glory   105
11. Winds of Change   123
12. A Time for Sowing   131
13. Storm Warnings   142
14. Flight   160
Epilogue   170

Foreword

My initial impression of Madame Bilquis Sheikh of Pakistan was of her large, expressive, luminous eyes. I saw pain written there, and compassion, and rare sensitivity to the world of the spirit.

A woman of mysterious age with hints of gray in her hair, she was wearing a beautiful sari with dignity and grace. There was about her the unmistakable aura of having been born to wealth and position. Her voice was the deepest with the most resonant timbre I have ever heard in a woman.

Our first meeting took place in the mirrored dining room of a Bel Air, California, restaurant. That day I heard the outline of Madame Sheikh's amazing story. Many another's adventure can perhaps equal hers in dramatic content, but few in one respect: only rarely does the sovereign God interrupt the flow of history to reach down and reveal Himself to a human being in such unmistakable fashion as He did with her. The element of initiative from the Godward side was so startling as to be reminiscent of Saul of Tarsus' experience on the road to Damascus. As I heard the recital of these extraordinary events, I knew then that this story must be given to the world.

Two years have passed since that first meeting. I could not

have known that day that Bilquis Sheikh was to become not only a cherished friend, but a veritable mother in the Lord to me.

As the events unfolded that knit our lives together, I discovered a woman who knows but one passion—to be a catalyst to mediate the Lord she loves to each hungry heart she encounters. To make this possible the same Lord has given her His special gifts of spiritual perception along with the gift of knowledge.

One day in October, 1976, Bilquis telephoned me in Florida from her home in California. "I pick up the spirit that you are troubled about something. What is it? And how can I help?"

I was astonished at this perception. "You're right, I *am* troubled," I told her. "I've just learned that I must have a major operation. The doctor strikes me as something of an alarmist, but—"

After gathering all the facts, Madame Sheikh said that she would seek Jesus' word on this—and hung up. By then I knew that whenever my friend said she would pray about something, that meant that she would be down on her knees before Him, sometimes for hours.

The next day she called back. Over the miles the deep voice spoke reassurance. "You have nothing at all to fear. The operation will go smoothly in all respects, and the surgeon will find everything benign."

And that's exactly the way it turned out.

At another time Bilquis telephoned Dick and Betty Schneider in Virginia. Though Dick was working steadily on the manuscript of *I Dared To Call Him Father*, he had had no personal contact with Madame Sheikh for a number of days. "Something is wrong there with you two," she began. "There is some emergency. Tell me about it, dear friends."

There was indeed! The Schneiders have two sons in college. One of them had been viciously beaten up after he had protested seeing three burly upperclassmen physically assaulting a smaller, bespectacled student. The dormitory situation was now worrisome, school authorities had not been fully apprised, and there was the danger of the Schneiders' son wanting to leave school.

In this instance Madame Sheikh was able to get God's directions on the wise way to handle the problem, and it was resolved happily.

At such times I have marveled that a new Christian could have such depth of perception into the world of spirit. Also, how odd that God would reach down for a Muslim woman in Pakistan to bring her to minister in the United States! Could it be that the eastern heritage and psyche is generally more fertile soil for spiritual understanding than that of western man?

Beyond that, the intensity of Madame Sheikh's passion to witness for her Lord has fulfilled God's primary condition for bestowing His special gifts of the Holy Spirit. These gifts, with the unction and authority that come with them, are very apparent to all who hear her speak across the country. Yet the fact that she fits no established pattern puzzles many who are more comfortable when any given leader can be tagged.

One Christian leader demanded in a letter that she state whether or not she was a Charismatic. She sat at her desk thinking about this question and how even a single word can divide those who love Christ. Playfully, on impulse she picked up a quarter from her purse and said, "Well, Father, You decide."

She flipped the quarter into the air saying, "Heads, I'm Charismatic; tails, I'm not." The silver coin spun blithely in the air, then dropped to her carpet. She could scarcely believe what she saw. Kneeling down to make certain, she chuckled. What better proof could she have of the Lord's sense of humor?

The quarter had landed on its edge in the thick folds and was standing straight up.

The lesson, Bilquis says, is that the important thing is not *how* we worship or what words we use, or what tags we tie on, but do we love our neighbors? Are we guided by His Holy Spirit? Do we obey Him implicitly? Do we weep for those who do not know Christ? Do we long to share our knowledge of Him?

Madame Sheikh has found in America a surprising hunger for Jesus. Surprising to her because in a vision she had had in Pakistan before emigrating to this country, she had seen America as a land of many churches, their steeples rising above every town and city. She had assumed from this that America must be a land completely devoted to God.

But then in the vision there had also been a flock of hungry white geese. After traveling the length and breadth of the country, she now knows that the geese represented all those in this land who have not heard of Him.

Vividly, she described to us her first Sunday in the United States. . . . She had stepped out of her hotel to see the streets filled with traffic. "They must all be on their way to church," she thought. She was to learn, however, that most of these people were on their way to the beaches, golf courses, and picnic grounds.

It is for these people that Madame Sheikh yearns as well as for the future of this nation.

In a sense she is now a woman without a country, partly because she has God's broad perspective on our world. In another sense she carries her beloved Pakistan with her wherever she goes. Having had to leave behind her little plot of earth on the other side of the world with her garden, she has been busy creating another one on the hillside behind the little house in California which she shares with her grandson Mahmud. So beautiful has that little garden become that neighbors on her street who had given up on the barren hillside behind their homes, inspired by Madame Sheikh, are now creating their own gardens.

Bilquis told me how as she worked amongst her flowers recently, she was thinking about the English missionary

William Carey with whom she had come to feel very close, even though he died 143 years ago in India.

He loved the English daisies which bloomed in the meadows of his home town of Paulerspury, Northamptonshire. In his later years in India, some friends sent him a few seeds of his favorite flower, and Madame Sheikh has carefully copied into her journal the letter he wrote at that time:

> I shook the bag over a patch of earth in a shady place. On visiting the spot a few days afterwards, to my inexpressible delight, I found a *bellis perennis* of our English pastures springing up. I do not know that I ever enjoyed, since leaving Europe, a simple pleasure so exquisite as the sight of this English daisy afforded me, having not seen one for thirty years and never expecting to see one again.

Bilquis Sheikh wept when she first read that letter. She finds the flowers in the United States very lovely, with many of them the same kinds that grew in her gardens in Wah. But there remains that residue of nostalgia for her homeland. She keeps hoping to see certain of the Wah flowers that do not grow here; keeps hoping that someday someone in Pakistan will send *her* some seeds too.

Meanwhile, we in the United States are richer for her presence among us. Each time I am with her, each time I hear her deep voice over the phone, I am reassured that God is still a sovereign God, that He is still in control of our world.

CATHERINE MARSHALL

Evergreen Farm, Virginia
October 15, 1977

1.

A Frightening Presence

The strange prickly feeling grew inside me as I walked slowly along the graveled paths of my garden. It was deep twilight. The scent of late narcissus hung heavy in the air. What was it, I wondered, that made me so uneasy?

I stopped my walk and looked around. Inside my home some distance across the broad lawn the servants were beginning to flick on lights in the dining area. Outside all seemed peaceful and quiet. I reached out to snip off some of the pungent white blossoms for my bedroom. As I leaned over to grasp the tall green stems, something brushed past my head.

I straightened in alarm. What was it? A mist-like cloud— a cold, damp unholy presence—had floated by. The garden suddenly seemed darker. A chilling breeze sprang up through the weeping willows and I shivered.

Get hold of yourself, Bilquis! I scolded. My imagination was playing tricks on me. Nevertheless, I gathered my flowers and headed quickly toward the house where windows glowed in warm reassurance. Its sturdy white stone walls and oaken doors offered protection. As I hurried along the crunchy gravel path I found myself glancing over my shoulder. I had always laughed at talk of the supernatural. Of course there wasn't anything out there. Was there?

As if in answer, I felt a firm, very real and uncanny tap on my right hand.

I screamed. I rushed into the house and slammed the door behind me. My servants ran to me, afraid to make any comment at all, for I must have looked like a ghost myself. It wasn't until bedtime that I finally found the courage to speak to my two handmaids about the cold presence. "Do you believe in spiritual things?" I asked, on concluding my story. Both Nur-jan and Raisham, one a Muslim, the other a Christian, avoided answering my question but Nur-jan, her hands fluttering nervously, asked me if she could call the village *mullah*, a priest from the mosque, who would bring some holy water to cleanse the garden. But my common sense had returned and I rebelled at submitting to the superstition of the ignorant. Besides, I didn't want any word of this to spread in the village. I tried to smile at her concern, and told her, a little too abruptly I'm afraid, that I didn't want any holy man on my grounds pretending to remove evil spirits. Nevertheless, after the maids left the room, I found myself picking up my copy of the Koran. But after struggling through a few pages of the Muslim Holy Book, I wearied of it, slipped it back within its blue silken case, and fell asleep.

I slowly awakened the next morning like a swimmer struggling to the surface, a thin high chant piercing my consciousness:

"Laa ilaaha illa Ilaah,
Muhammed resolu'lla!"

The sing-song words drifted through the filigree of my bedroom window:

"There is no God but Allah:
And Muhammed is his Prophet."

It was a comforting sound, this Muslim call to prayer because it seemed so utterly normal after the previous night.

It was a call I had heard almost without exception every morning of my 46 years. I envisioned the source of the rolling chant.

Some moments before in the little nearby Pakistani village of Wah, our old muezzin had hurried through the door at the base of an ancient minaret. Inside its cool interior he had trudged up curving stone steps worn smooth by the sandals of generations of Muslim holy men. At the top of the prayer tower, I could imagine him hesitating at the carved teak door leading to the parapet to catch his breath. Then, stepping outside to the railing, he threw back his bearded head and in syllables fourteen hundred years old called the faithful to prayer.

> *"Come to prayer, come to salvation,*
> *Prayer is better than sleep."*

The haunting cry floated through the morning mist across cobblestone lanes in Wah still cold from the October night, drifted across my garden to curl along the house's old stone walls now ruddy in the light of the rising sun.

As the last wisps of the ancient chant hung above me, I remembered the eerie experience in the garden the night before, and quickly turned to morning routines that would be comforting just because they were so ordinary. I sat up and reached for the golden bell on my marble bedside table. At its musical tinkle, my maid Nur-jan hurried in out of breath as usual. Both of my handmaids slept in a room adjoining mine and I knew that they had already been up for an hour, waiting for my call. Morning tea in my bed was a *must*. Nur-jan began laying out my silver brushes and combs. She was a willing teen-aged girl, plump and giggly, but a bit clumsy. When she dropped a brush, I scolded her sharply.

Raisham, my other handmaid, older and quieter, a tall graceful woman, slid into the room bearing a large covered tea tray. She placed it on my bed table, drew back the

white linen to expose the sterling service and poured me
a cup of steaming tea.

Sipping the scalding ambrosia, I sighed in satisfaction; tea
was better than prayer. My mother would have been
shocked at my thought. How many times had I watched
her place her prayer rug on the tiled bedroom floor, then,
facing the holy city of Mecca, kneel and press her forehead
to the rug in prayer. Thinking of my mother I looked over
to the dressing case on my table. Fashioned centuries ago
of sandalwood and covered with engraved sterling silver, it
had belonged to Mother and her mother before her. Now it
was my heirloom to treasure. After finishing two cups of
tea I leaned forward, a sign for Raisham to begin brushing
my graying waist-length hair while Nur-jan carefully worked
on my nails.

As the two worked, they gossiped in easy familiarity about
news from the village, Nur-jan chattering and Raisham
making quiet thoughtful comments. They talked about a
boy who was leaving home for the city and a girl soon to
be married. And then they discussed the murder that happened in a nearby town where Raisham's aunt lived. I could
sense Raisham shudder as the news came up. For the victim
had been a Christian. She was a young girl who had been
staying in a Christian missionary's home. Someone had
stumbled across her body in one of the narrow lanes criss-
crossing her village. There was supposed to have been an
investigation by the constabulary.

"Any news about the girl?" I casually asked.

"No, Begum Sahib," said Raisham quietly, as she carefully began to work a braid in my hair. I could understand
why Raisham, a Christian herself, didn't want to talk about
the murder. She knew as well as I did who had killed that
girl. After all, the girl had forsaken her Muslim faith to be
baptized a Christian. So the brother, infuriated by the
shame this sin had brought upon his family, had obeyed
the ancient law of the faithful that those who fall away from
their faith must be slain.

Even though Muslim edicts may be stern and harsh, their interpretations are sometimes tempered with mercy and compassion. But there are always the zealots who carry out the letter of the Koran law to the extreme.

Everyone knew who had killed the girl. But nothing would be done. It had always been this way. A year ago, the Christian servant of one of the missionaries ended up in a ditch, his throat cut, and nothing had been done there either. I put the sad little story out of my mind and made ready to get up. My maids hurried to the closet and returned with several silken saris for my selection. I pointed to a jewel-embroidered one and after they helped drape it about me, they quietly bowed themselves out of my chamber.

Sunlight now flooded my bedroom, giving its white walls and ivory-colored furnishings a saffron glow. The sunlight glinted from a gold-framed photograph on my dressing table and I stepped over and picked it up, angry, because I had put the picture face down the day before; one of the servants must have set it up again! The engraved frame enclosed a photograph of a sophisticated-looking couple smiling at me from a corner table in a luxurious London restaurant.

In spite of myself I looked at the picture again, as one does when he keeps pressing a hurting tooth. The dashing man with dark mustache and burning eyes had been my husband, General Khalid Sheikh. Why did I keep this picture! Hate surged within me as I looked at the man I once felt I could not live without. When the photo had been taken six years before, Khalid had been Pakistan's Minister of Interior.

The glamorous-looking woman next to him had been me. As daughter of a conservative Muslim family which for seven hundred years had been landed gentry in this cool-climated Northwest Frontier Province of what had once been northern India, I had been hostess to diplomats and industrialists from all over the world. I had been accustomed to sojourns in Paris and London where I spent my time shopping on the Rue de la Paix or in Harrods. The lithsome woman who smiled from the photo no longer existed, I thought as I looked in the mirror. The soft pale skin had bronzed, the lustrous black hair was now streaked with gray, and disillusionment had etched deep lines in her face.

The world of the photograph had crumbled into fragments five years before when Khalid left me. Suffering the shame of rejection, I had fled the sophisticated life of London, Paris and Rawalpindi to seek refuge here in the quiet peace of my family's ancestral estate nestled at the foot of the Himalayan Mountains. The estate comprised the little hill country village of Wah where I had spent so many happy days as a child. Wah was surrounded by gardens and orchards which many generations of my family had planted. And the big stone palatial home with its towers, terraces and huge echoing chambers seemed as old as the snow-crowned Safed Koh mountains which loomed in the west. However, my aunt also lived in this house and desiring further seclusion, I moved to a smaller house the family had built on the outskirts of Wah. Inset like a jewel in twelve acres of gardens, this house, with bedrooms upstairs and living, dining and drawing rooms downstairs, promised the solace I needed.

It gave me more. For when I arrived, much of the extensive gardens had become overgrown. This was a blessing, for I buried much of my sorrow in the lush soil as I plunged into the restoration of the grounds. I made some of the twelve acres into formal gardens with walls and flower beds and left some of the area natural. Slowly the gardens, with their countless musical springs, became my world until by then, in the year 1966, I had the reputation of a recluse who secluded herself outside of town nestled amongst her flowers.

I looked away from the gold-framed photo in my hand, placed it face down again on the table and turned to my bedroom window looking toward the village. Wah . . . the very name of the village was an exclamation of joy. Cen-

turies before, when this was but a hamlet, the legendary
Moghul emperor Akbar traveled through here and his
caravan stopped to rest by a spring in what was now my
surroundings. He gratefully sank down under a willow, and
exclaimed in joy, "Wah!" thus naming the area forever.

But the memory of this scene gave me no release from
the unsettled feeling which had been hovering over me
ever since the strange experience of the evening before.

However, I tried to dispel it as I stood at my window. It
was morning again, I told myself, the next day, a safe time
with familiar routines and warm sunlight. The previous
night's episode seemed as real, but as remote, as a bad
dream. I drew the white drapes aside and breathed in
deeply of the fresh morning air, listening to the hissing of
the sweeper's broom on the patio. A fragrance of wood
smoke from early morning cooking fires drifted up to me
and the rhythmic thumping of water-mill wheels sounded
in the distance. I sighed in satisfaction. This was Wah, this
was my home, this was, after all, safety. This was where
Nawab Muhammad Hayat Kahn, a prince and feudal landowner, had lived seven hundred years ago. We were his
direct descendants and my family was known throughout
India as the Hayats of Wah. Centuries ago the caravans of
emperors would turn off the Grand Trunk Road to visit my
ancestors. Even in my earlier days notables from all over
Europe and Asia would take the same road, once an ancient
caravan route across India, to see my family. But now,
usually only members of my family would follow it to my
gate. Of course this meant that I didn't see many people
who were not part of my immediate household. I did not
much care. My fourteen house servants were enough company. They and their ancestors had served my family for
generations. Most important, I had Mahmud.

Mahmud was my four-year-old grandson. His mother,
Tooni, was the youngest of my three children. A slim at-
tractive woman, Tooni was a medical doctor at Holy Family
Hospital in nearby Rawalpindi. Her former husband was a

prominent landlord. However, they had an unhappy marriage and their relationship deteriorated a little each year. During their long bitter disagreements, Tooni would send Mahmud to visit me until she and her husband reached another uneasy truce. One day, Tooni and her husband came to see me. Could I keep one-year-old Mahmud for a while until they settled their differences?

"No," I said. "I do not want him to become a tennis ball. But I will be willing to adopt him and raise him as my own son." Sadly, Tooni and her husband never could settle their differences and they finally divorced. However, they did approve my adopting Mahmud, and it was working out quite well. Tooni came to see Mahmud often and the three of us were very close, particularly since my two other children lived far away.

Later that morning Mahmud pedaled his tricycle across the brick terrace shaded by almond trees. He had been with me for over three years and this lively cherubic child with deep brown eyes and button nose was the only joy of my life. His pealing laughter seemed to lift the spirit of this secluded old house. Even so I worried about how he would be affected by living with such a downcast person as me. I tried to compensate by making sure his every need was anticipated, and this included his own staff of three servants, in addition to my own eleven, to dress him, bring out his toys and pick them up when he was through playing with them.

But I was troubled about Mahmud. For several days he had refused to eat. This was particularly strange, for the boy was always visiting the bake kitchen to cajole my cooks into giving him sugar biscuits and snacks. Earlier that morning I had gone downstairs, walked through the terrazzo entranceway out to the terrace. After exchanging a warm hug with Mahmud, I asked his servant if the child had eaten.

"No, Begum Sahib, he refuses," the maid said in a near

whisper. When I pressed Mahmud to take some food, he just answered that he was not hungry.

I was really disturbed when Nur-jan came to me alone and suggested timorously that Mahmud was being attacked by evil spirits. Startled, I looked at her sharply, remembering the disquieting experience of the night before. What did all this mean? Once again I asked Mahmud to eat, but to no avail. He wouldn't even touch his favorite Swiss chocolates which I had imported especially for him. His limpid eyes looked up to me when I offered him the package. "I'd love to eat them, Mum," he said, "but when I try to swallow it hurts." A cold chill ran through me as I looked at my little grandson, once so lively and now so listless.

I immediately summoned Manzur, my chauffeur, also a Christian, and ordered him to get the car out. Within an hour we were in Rawalpindi to visit Mahmud's doctor. The pediatrician examined Mahmud carefully and he reported that he could find nothing wrong.

Fear chilled me as we rode back to the estate. Looking at my little grandson sitting quietly beside me, I wondered. Could Nur-jan *possibly* be right? Was this something that went beyond the physical? Was it . . . something in the spirit world attacking him? I reached over and put my arm around the child, smiling at myself for entertaining such ideas. Once, I remembered, my father had told me about a legendary Muslim holy man who could perform miracles. I laughed aloud at the idea. My father was displeased, but that was the way I felt about any such claims. Still, today, holding Mahmud close as the car turned off the Grand Trunk Road onto our lane, I found myself toying with an unwelcome thought: Could Mahmud's problem be related to the mist in the garden?

When I shared my fears with Nur-jan, her henna-tipped fingers flew to her throat and she begged me to call the village *mullah* and ask him to pray for Mahmud and sprinkle holy water over the garden.

I debated her request. Even though I believed in basic

Muslim teachings, for several years I had drifted away from the many rituals, the praying five times a day, the fasting, the complicated ceremonial washings. But my concern for Mahmud overcame my doubts and I told Nur-jan that she could call the holy man from the village mosque.

The next morning Mahmud and I sat at my window impatiently awaiting the *mullah*. When I finally saw him making his way up the steps of the veranda, his thin ragged coat flapping about him in the chilling fall wind, I was both sorry I had asked him and angry that he wasn't walking faster.

Nur-jan brought the bony old man to my quarters, then withdrew. Mahmud watched the man curiously as he opened his Koran. The *mullah*, whose skin matched the ancient leather of his holy book, looked at me through crinkled eyes, laid a gnarled brown hand on Mahmud's head and in a quavering voice began reciting the Kul. This is the prayer every Muslim recites when he is about to begin any important act, whether to pray for the sick or to enter a business agreement.

The *mullah* then started to read from the Koran in Arabic —the Koran is always read in Arabic since it would be wrong to translate the very words that God's angel had given the prophet Muhammad. I became impatient. I must have started to tap my foot.

"Begum Sahib?" the *mullah* said, holding the Koran out to me. "You, too, should read these verses." He referred to the Sura Falak and Sura Naz, verses to be repeated when one is troubled. "Why don't you repeat these verses as well?"

"No," I said, "I will not. God has forgotten about me and I have forgotten about God!" But at the hurt look on the old man's face I softened. After all, he had come here at my request and with Mahmud's welfare in mind. "All right," I said, taking the worn volume. I let it fall open, then read the first verse my eyes fell on:

*Muhammad is the Messenger of God, and those who
are with him are hard against the unbelievers. . . .*

I thought of the Christian girl who had been murdered,
and about the mist that appeared in my garden shortly
after she was killed, and above all about Mahmud's mysterious ailment. Could they be related? Surely any angry
spiritual power would never link me and Mahmud with a
Christian. I shuddered.

But the holy man seemed satisfied. Despite my reserva-
tions he returned for three days in a row to recite verses
over Mahmud.

And, just to complete the series of mysterious, unsettling
events, Mahmud did get better.

How was I supposed to think about all these happenings?

I was soon to find out. For without knowing it, events
had been set in motion which would shatter the world I'd
known all my life.

2.

The Strange Book

After these experiences I found myself drawn to the Koran.
Perhaps it would help explain the events and at the same
time fill the emptiness within me. Certainly its curved
Arabic script held answers which had often sustained my
family.

I had read the Koran before of course. I remembered
exactly how old I was when I first started learning Arabic
so that I could read our holy book: I was four years, four
months and four days old. This was the day every Muslim
child began to unravel the Arabic script. The moment was
marked by a great family banquet, to which all my relatives
came. It was then, in a special ceremony, that the wife of
our village *mullah* began teaching me the alphabet.

I especially remember my Uncle Fateh (we children
called him Grand Uncle Fateh; he wasn't really my uncle—
all older kinsmen are called Uncle or Aunt in Pakistan).
Grand Uncle Fateh was the relative closest to our family,
and I remember clearly how he watched me at the ceremony, his sensitive aquiline face glowing with pleasure as I
heard again the story of how the angel Gabriel began
giving Muhammad the words of the Koran on that fateful
"Night of Power" in the year 610 A.D. It took me seven years
to read the holy book through for the first time but when I

finally finished, there was cause for yet another family celebration.

Always before, I had read the Koran as an obligation. This time, I felt I should really search its pages. I took my copy, which had belonged to my mother, relaxed on the white eiderdown coverlet of my bed, and began to read. I started with the initial verse, the first message given to the young prophet Muhammad as he sat by himself in a cave on Mount Hira:

> *Recite: In the name of thy Lord who created,*
> *Created Man of a blood clot.*
> *Recite: And thy Lord is the Most Generous,*
> *Who taught by the Pen,*
> *Taught man that he knew not.*

At first I was lost in the beauty of the words. But later on in the book there were words that did not comfort me at all:

> *When ye have divorced women, and they have reached their term, then retain them in kindness or release them in kindness.*

My husband's eyes had been like black steel when he told me that he didn't love me any more. I shriveled inside as he spoke. What had happened to all our years together! Could they be dismissed just like that? Had I, as the Koran said, "reached my term"?

The next morning I picked up the Koran again, hoping to find in the curling script the assurance I needed so desperately. But the assurance never came. I found only directives for how to live and warnings against other beliefs. There were verses about the prophet Jesus whose message, the Koran said, was falsified by early Christians. Though Jesus was born of a virgin, he was not God's son. *So say not "Three,"* warned the Koran against the Christian concept of the Trinity. *Refrain; better is it for you. God is only One God.*

After several days of applying myself to the holy book, I put it down one afternoon with a sigh, got up and walked down to my garden where I hoped to find some peace in nature and in old memories. Even at this time of the year, the lush greenness persisted, brightened here and there by colorful alyssum which still blossomed. It was a warm day for fall and Mahmud skipped along the paths where I had walked as a child with my father. I could picture Father now, walking beside me here, wearing his white turban, impeccably dressed in his conservative British suit from Saville Row as befitted a government minister. Often he would call me by my full name, Bilquis Sultana, knowing how much I enjoyed hearing it. For Bilquis was the first name of the Queen of Sheba and everyone knew Sultana signified royalty.

We had many good conversations. And in later years we enjoyed talking about our new country, Pakistan. He was so proud of it. "The Islamic Republic of Pakistan was created especially as a homeland for South Asian Muslims," he said. "We're one of the largest countries under Islamic law in the world," he added, pointing out that 96% of our country's population was Muslim, with the rest made up mostly of scattered groups of Buddhists, Christians, and Hindus.

I sighed and looked up beyond my garden trees to the lavender hills in the distance. I could always find solace with my father. In his later years I had become a companion to him, often discussing our country's rapidly changing political situation with him and explaining my views. He was so gentle, so understanding. But now he was gone. I remembered standing by his open grave in the Muslim cemetery of Brookwood outside of London. He had travelled to London for surgery and had never recovered. Muslim custom requires that a body be buried within 24 hours of death and by the time I reached the cemetery his coffin was ready to be lowered into the grave. I couldn't believe I'd never see my father again. They unfastened the coffin lid so I could have one last look at him. But the cold gray clay in that box was not him; where had he gone? I stood there numbly wondering about it all as they refastened the coffin, each shrill squeal of the screws biting into the damp wood sending pain through me.

Mother, with whom I was also very close, died seven years later, leaving me completely alone.

There in my garden, shadows had lengthened and again I stood in twilight. No, the comfort I had sought in memories proved only to bring achings. Softly in the distance I could hear the muezzin's sunset prayer call; its haunting strains only deepened the loneliness within me.

"Where? Oh Allah," I whispered to the prayer rhythms, "*where* is the comfort You promise?"

Back in my bedroom that evening I again picked up my mother's copy of the Koran. And as I read I was again impressed by its many references to Jewish and Christian writings which preceded it. Perhaps, I wondered, I should continue my search among those earlier books?

But that would mean reading the Bible. How could the Bible help since, of course, as everyone knew, the early Christians had falsified so much of it. But the idea of reading the Bible became more and more insistent. What was the Bible's concept of God? What *did* it say about the prophet Jesus? Perhaps after all I should read it.

But then came the next problem: where would I get a Bible? No shops in our area would carry one.

Perhaps Raisham would have a copy. But I dismissed the thought. Even if she did, my request would frighten her. Pakistanis have been murdered for even appearing to persuade Muslims to turn traitor-Christian. I thought of my other Christian servants. My family warned that I should not employ Christian servants because of their notorious lack of loyalty and untrustworthiness. But I didn't let that bother me; as long as they could fulfill their duties, I was satisfied. Doubtless they weren't very sincere anyhow. After all, when the Christian missionaries came to India, they found it easy to make converts among the lower classes. Most of these were the sweepers, people so low in the social order that their work was limited to cleaning the streets, walks and gutters. We Muslims called these servile ones "rice Christians." Wasn't that the reason they accepted a false religion, mainly to get the food, clothes and schooling which the missionaries doled out?

We looked upon the missionaries themselves with amusement; they busied themselves so eagerly over these poor creatures. In fact, only a few months before, my chauffeur Manzur, a Christian, asked if he could show my garden to some local missionaries who had admired it through the fence.

"Of course," I said gratuitously, thinking of poor Manzur who evidently wanted so much to impress these people. A few days later from my drawing room window I watched the young American couple stroll through the garden. Manzur had referred to them as the Reverend and Mrs. David Mitchell. Both had pale brown hair, pale eyes and wore drab western clothes. What colorless creatures, I thought. Even so, I did pass word on to the gardener to give these missionaries some seeds if they wished them.

But thinking of them gave me my answer to getting a Bible. Manzur would get one for me. Tomorrow I would give him the assignment.

So I summoned him to my apartment the next morning. He stood at attention before me in his white pantaloons, the nervous twitch in his face making me uneasy, as it always did.

"Manzur, I want you to get me a Bible."

"A Bible?" his eyes widened.

"Of course!" I said, trying to be patient. Since Manzur didn't know how to read, I was sure he didn't own a Bible. But I felt he could get one for me. When he mumbled something I could not understand I repeated, simply but firmly, "Manzur, get me a Bible."

He nodded, bowed and left. I knew why he was resisting

my request. Manzur was made of no firmer stuff than Raisham. They were both remembering that murdered girl. Giving a Bible to a sweeper was one thing; bringing a Bible to a person of the upper classes was quite something else. Word of this could get him into deep trouble indeed.

Two days later Manzur was driving me to Rawalpindi to see Tooni.

"Manzur, I do not have the Bible as yet."

I could see his knuckles whiten on the steering wheel.

"Begum, I will get you one."

Three days later I summoned him to the house.

"Manzur, I have asked you to bring me a Bible three times, and you have not." The twitch in his face became more noticeable. "I'll give you one more day. If I do not have one by tomorrow you will be fired."

His face turned ashen. He knew I meant it. He wheeled and left, his chauffeur boots clicking on the terrazzo floor.

The next day just before a visit from Tooni, a little Bible mysteriously appeared on my downstairs drawing room table. I picked it up, and examined it closely. Cheaply bound in a gray cloth cover, it was printed in Urdu, a local Indian dialect. It had been translated by an Englishman 180 years before and I found the old-fashioned phraseology difficult to follow. Manzur had evidently got it from a friend; it was almost new. I leafed through its thin pages, set it down and forgot about it.

A few minutes later Tooni arrived. Mahmud ran in just behind her, squealing, because he knew his mother would have brought him a toy. In a minute Mahmud raced through the French doors to the terrace with his new airplane, and Tooni and I settled down to our tea.

It was then that Tooni noticed the Bible resting on the table near me. "Oh, a Bible!" she said. "Do open it and see what it has to say." Our family views any religious book as significant. It was a common pastime to allow a holy book to fall open, point blindly at a passage to see what it said, almost like having it give a prophecy.

Lightheartedly, I opened the little Bible and looked down at the pages.

Then, a mysterious thing happened. It was as if my attention were being drawn to a verse on the lower right hand corner of the right page. I bent close to read it:

> *I will call that my people, which was not my people; and her beloved, which was not beloved. And it shall be, that in the place where it was said unto them, Ye are not my people, there shall they be called sons of the living God.*
>
> Romans 9:25–26 *

I caught my breath and a tremor passed through me. Why was this verse affecting me so! *I will call that my people, which was not my people. . . . In the place where it was said unto them, Ye are not my people, there shall they be called sons of the living God.*

A silence hung over the room. I looked up to see Tooni poised expectantly, ready to hear what I had found. But I could not read the words out loud. Something in them was too profound for me to read as amusement.

"Well, what was it Mother?" asked Tooni, her alive eyes questioning me.

I closed the book, murmured something about this not being a game anymore, and turned the conversation to another subject.

But the words burned in my heart like glowing embers. And they turned out to be preparation for the most unusual dreams I have ever had.

---

* Modernized to Phillips' Translation

3.

The Dreams

It wasn't until the next day that I again picked up the little gray Bible. Neither Tooni nor I referred to the Bible again after I had switched the conversation to another subject. But throughout the long afternoon the words in that passage simmered just below the surface of my consciousness.

Early in the evening of the next day, I retired to my bedchamber where I planned to rest and meditate. I took the Bible with me and settled among the soft white cushions of my divan. Once again I leafed through its pages and read another puzzling passage:

> *But Israel, following the Law of righteousness, failed to reach the goal of righteousness.*
>
> Romans 9:31 *

Ah, I thought. Just as the Koran said; the Jews *had* missed the mark. The writer of these passages might have been a Muslim, I thought, for he continued to speak of the people of Israel as not knowing God's righteousness.

But the next passage made me catch my breath.

* Modernized to Phillips' Translation

> *For Christ means the end of the struggle for righteous-*
> *ness-by-the-Law for everyone who believes in him.*
>
> Romans 10:4 *

I lowered the book down for a moment. Christ? *He* was the end of the struggle? I continued on.

> *For the secret is very near you, in your own heart, in*
> *your own mouth. . . . If you openly admit by your*
> *own mouth that Jesus Christ is the Lord, and if you*
> *believe in your own heart that God raised him from the*
> *dead, you will be saved.*
>
> Romans 10:8–9 *

I put the book down again, shaking my head. This directly contradicted the Koran. Muslims knew the prophet Jesus was just human, that the man did not die on the cross but was whisked up to heaven by God and a look-alike put on the cross instead. Now sojourning in an inferior heaven, this Jesus will someday return to earth to reign for forty years, marry, have children, and then die. In fact, I heard that there is a special grave plot kept vacant for the man's remains in Medina, the city where Muhammad is also buried. At the Resurrection Day, Jesus will rise and stand with other men to be judged before God Almighty. But this Bible said Christ was raised from the dead. It was either blasphemy or. . . .

My mind whirled. I knew that whoever called upon the name of Allah would be saved. But to believe that Jesus Christ *is* Allah? Even Muhammad, the final and greatest of the messengers of God, the *Seal of the Prophets*, was only a mortal.

I lay back on my bed, my hand over my eyes. If the Bible and Koran represent the same God, why is there so much confusion and contradiction? How could it be the same God if the God of the Koran is one of vengeance and punishment and the God of the Christian Bible is one of mercy and forgiveness? I don't know when I fell asleep.

* Modernized to Phillips' Translation

Normally I never dream, but this night I did. The dream was so lifelike, the events in it so real, that I found it difficult the next morning to believe they were only fantasy. Here is what I saw.

> *I found myself having supper with a man I knew to be Jesus. He had come to visit me in my home and stayed for two days. He sat across the table from me and in peace and joy we ate dinner together. Suddenly, the dream changed. Now I was on a mountain top with another man. He was clothed in a robe and shod with sandals. How was it that I mysteriously knew his name, too? John the Baptist. What a strange name. I found myself telling this John the Baptist about my recent visit with Jesus. "The Lord came and was my guest for two days," I said. "But now He is gone. Where is He? I must find Him! Perhaps you, John the Baptist, will lead me to Him?"*

That was the dream. When I woke up I was loudly calling the name, "John the Baptist! John the Baptist!" Nur-jan and Raisham rushed into my room. They seemed embarrassed at my shouting and began fussily to prepare my toilette. I tried to tell them about my dream as they worked.

"Oh, how nice," giggled Nur-jan as she presented my tray of perfumes. "Yes, it was a blessed dream," murmured Raisham as she brushed my hair. I was surprised that as a Christian, Raisham wouldn't be more excited. I started to ask her about John the Baptist but checked myself; after all, Raisham was just a simple village woman. But who *was* this John the Baptist? I had not come across the name in what I had read so far in the Bible.

For the next three days I continued reading both the Bible and the Koran side by side, turning from one to the other. I found myself picking up the Koran out of a sense of duty, and then eagerly turning to the Christian book, dipping into it here and there to look into this confusing new world I had discovered. Each time I opened the Bible a sense of guilt filled me. Perhaps this stemmed from my strict unbringing. Even after I had become a young woman, Father would have to approve any book I read. Once my brother and I smuggled a book into our room. Even though it was completely innocent, we were quite frightened, reading it.

Now as I opened the Bible, I found myself reacting in the same manner. One story riveted my attention. It told of the Jewish leaders bringing a woman caught in adultery to the prophet Jesus. I shivered, knowing what fate lay in store for this woman. The moral codes of the ancient east were not very different from ours in Pakistan. The men of the community are bound by tradition to punish the adulterous woman. As I read of the woman in the Bible standing before her accusers, I knew that her own brothers, uncles and cousins stood in the forefront, ready to stone her.

Then the Prophet said: *Let him who is without sin cast the first stone* (John 8:7).

I reeled as in my mind's eye I watched the men slink away. Instead of supervising her lawful death, Jesus had forced her accusers to recognize their own guilt. The book fell into my lap as I lay there deep in thought. There was something so logical, so right about this prophet's challenge. The man spoke truth.

Then three days later I had a second strange dream:

> *I was in the bedchamber when a maid announced that a perfume salesman was waiting to see me. I arose from my divan elated, for at this time there was a shortage of imported perfumes in Pakistan. I greatly feared running low on my favorite luxury. And so in my dream I happily asked my maid to show the perfume salesman in.*
>
> *He was dressed in the manner of perfume salesmen in my mother's day when these merchants travelled from house to house selling their wares. He wore a black frock coat and carried his stock in a valise. Opening the valise, he took out a golden jar. Removing the cap, he handed it to me. As I looked at it I caught my breath; the perfume glimmered like liquid crystal. I was about to touch my finger to it when he held up his hand.*

"No," he said. Taking the golden jar he walked over and placed it on my bedside table. "This will spread throughout the world," he said.

As I awakened in the morning, the dream was still vivid in my mind. The sun was streaming through the window, and I could still smell that beautiful perfume; its delightful fragrance filled the room. I raised up and looked at my bedside table, half expecting to see the golden jar there.

Instead, where the jar had been, now rested the Bible!

A tingle passed through me. I sat on the edge of the bed pondering my two dreams. What did they mean? Where I had not dreamed in years, now I had two vivid dreams in a row. Were they related to each other? And were they related to my recent brush with the realities of the supernatural world?

That afternoon I went for my usual stroll in the garden. I was still bemused by my dreams. But now something else was added. It was as if I felt a strange delight and joy, a peace beyond anything I had ever known before. It was as if I were close to the Presence of God. Suddenly, as I stepped out of a grove into a sun-flooded open area, the air around me seemed to be alive with another lovely fragrance. It wasn't the fragrance of flowers—it was too late for any of the garden to be in bloom—but a very real fragrance nonetheless.

In some agitation I returned to the house. Where did that fragrance come from? What was happening to me? Who could I talk to about what was happening to me? It would have to be someone with a knowledge of the Bible. I had already swept aside the thought of asking my Christian servants. In the first place it was unthinkable to ask information of them. They probably had never even read the Bible and wouldn't know what I was talking about. No, I had to talk to someone who was educated and who knew this book.

As I considered this question a shocking idea came to

mind. I fought the thought. That would be the last place I should go for help.

But a name kept returning to me so compellingly that I finally rang for Manzur.

"I want you to get the car out for me." And then as an afterthought I added: "I'll be driving myself."

Manzur's eyes widened. "Yourself?"

"Yes, myself, if you please." He left, reluctantly. Rarely had I taken my car out that late in the evening. I had been an officer in the Royal Indian Army women's division in World War II and had driven ambulances and staff cars thousands of miles over all kinds of terrain. But wartime was one thing and even then I was in the company of someone. The daughter of Nawab nobility was not expected to drive her own car in normal life, especially not at night.

But I knew I couldn't risk Manzur knowing what I was about to do and resultant servants' gossip. I was convinced there was only one source where I could find the answer to my questions: Who was John the Baptist? What was this fragrance all about?

So it was with extreme reluctance that evening that I headed for the home of a couple I barely knew, the Reverend and Mrs. David Mitchell who had visited my garden that summer. As Christian missionaries, they were the last people with whom I'd want to be seen.

4.

The Encounter

My black Mercedes idled in the driveway. Manzur stood at the driver's door which he kept closed until the last moment protecting the car's warmth against the chill of that autumn evening. His dark eyes were still questioning my decision, but without comment. I got into the warm car, settled behind the wheel and drove off into the twilight, the Bible on the seat beside me.

Everyone knew where everyone else lived in this village of Wah. The Mitchells' home stood near the entrance of the Wah cement works from which my family derived part of its income. It served as the center of a strange little community about five miles outside of town. The homes had been built as temporary quarters for British troops during World War II. I recalled from the few times I had ventured into the area that the drab, uniform houses had lost most of their whitewash; their tin roofs showed signs of much patchwork. A strange mixture of expectancy and fear filled me as I drove along. I had never been in a Christian missionary home before. I was hopeful of learning the identity of my mystery man, John the Baptist, and yet I feared a certain—what should I call it, "influence?"—from those who might answer my question.

What would my forebears think of this visit to a Christian

missionary? I thought, for instance, of my great-grandfather who had accompanied the famed British General Nicholson through the Khyber Pass in one of the Afghanistan wars. What shame this visit would bring on my family. We had always associated the missionaries with the poor and social outcasts. I imagined a conversation with an uncle or aunt in which I defended myself by telling them of my strange dreams. "After all," I said in the scene I was playing out in my mind, "anyone would want to find out the meaning of such vivid dreams."

As I approached the Mitchells' area in the dim light of early evening, it was just as I remembered it, except that the look-alike bungalows seemed, if possible, even more drab. After searching up and down narrow lanes, I found the Mitchells' house near the cement works, just where I thought it would be, a small whitewashed bungalow, sitting in a grove of mulberry trees. As a precaution I started to park some distance away until I caught myself. I was being far too afraid of what my family thought. So I parked squarely in front of the Mitchells', picked up the Bible and moved quickly toward the house. The yard, I noticed, was neat and the screened veranda well maintained. At least these missionaries kept their place in good repair.

Suddenly, the house door opened and a group of chattering village women filed out, dressed in the typical *shalwar qamiz*, a loose pajama-like cotton outfit, with a *dupatta* (scarf). I stiffened. They would know me of course; nearly everyone in Wah recognized me. Now the story would be gossiped all over the area that Begum Sheikh had visited a Christian missionary!

And sure enough as soon as the women saw me in the light that came from the Mitchells' open front door, their chatter ceased abruptly. They hurried past me to the street, each touching hand to forehead in the traditional salute. There was nothing I could do but continue toward the door where Mrs. Mitchell stood staring out into the dusk. Up close she looked just as I remembered her, from seeing her at a distance about town, young, pale, almost fragile. Only now she was wearing a *shalwar qamiz* like the village women. As soon as she saw me her mouth fell open. "Why . . . why, Begum Sheikh!" she exclaimed, "What? . . . But. . . . Come in," she said. "Come in."

I was glad enough to step inside the house, away from the village women's eyes which I knew would be fixed on my back. We went into the living room, small and simply furnished. Mrs. Mitchell drew up what appeared to be the most comfortable chair for me near the open fire. She herself did not sit down, but stood folding and unfolding her hands. I glanced at a circle of chairs in the middle of the room. Mrs. Mitchell explained that she had just completed a Bible study with some local women. She gave a nervous cough. "Uh, will you have some tea?" she said, brushing back her hair.

"No thank you," I replied. "I have come to ask a question." I looked about. "Is the Reverend Mr. Mitchell here?"

"No. He is on a trip to Afghanistan."

I was sorry. The woman standing before me was so young! Would she be able to answer my questions?

"Mrs. Mitchell," I ventured, "do you know anything about God?"

She sank down into one of the wooden chairs and looked at me strangely; the only noise in the room was the low hiss from the flames in the fireplace. Then she said quietly, "I'm afraid I don't know too much *about* God, but I do *know* Him."

What an extraordinary statement! How could a person presume to know God! Just the same, the woman's odd confidence gave me confidence too. Before I quite knew what was happening, I found myself telling her about my dream of the prophet Jesus and the man named John the Baptist. Strangely, I had difficulty controlling my voice as I related the experience. Even as I told her, I felt the same excitement I felt on that mountain top. Then, after describing the dream, I leaned forward.

"Mrs. Mitchell, I've heard about Jesus, but *who* is John the Baptist?"

Mrs. Mitchell blinked at me and frowned. I felt she wanted to ask if I had really never heard of John the Baptist, but instead she settled back again in her chair. "Well, Begum Sheikh, John the Baptist was a prophet, a forerunner of Jesus Christ, who preached repentance and was sent to prepare the way for Him. He was the one who pointed to Jesus and said: 'Look, the Lamb of God who takes away the sins of the world.' He was the one who baptized Jesus."

Why did my heart skip at the word "baptized?" I knew little about these Christians, but all Muslims had heard of their strange ceremony of baptism. My mind flitted to the many people who were murdered after their baptisms. And this also happened under British rule when supposedly there was freedom of religion. Even as a child I had put the two facts together: a Muslim was baptized, a Muslim died.

"Begum Sheikh?"

I looked up. How long had we been sitting there silently? "Mrs. Mitchell," I said, my throat tight, "forget I am a Muslim. Just tell me: what did you mean when you said you know God?"

"I know Jesus," Mrs. Mitchell said and I knew she thought she was answering my question.

Then she told me what God had done for her and for the world by breaking the dreadful deadlock between sinful man and Himself by personally visiting this earth in the flesh, as Jesus, and dying for all of us on the cross.

The room was quiet again. I could hear trucks passing on the nearby highway. Mrs. Mitchell seemed in no hurry to speak. Finally, hardly believing my own ears, I took a breath and heard myself saying quite distinctly, "Mrs. Mitchell, some peculiar things have been happening at our house lately. Events of the spirit. Good and bad, both. I feel as if I were in the midst of an immense tug of war, and I need all the positive help I can get. Could you pray for me?"

The woman appeared startled at my request, then, collecting herself, she asked if I wanted to stand up, kneel or sit down as we prayed. I shrugged, suddenly horrified. All were equally unthinkable. But there was this slender, youthful woman kneeling on the floor of her bungalow. And I followed her!

"Oh Spirit of God," said Mrs. Mitchell in a soft voice, "I know that nothing I can say will convince Begum Sheikh who Jesus is. But I thank You that You take the veil off our eyes and reveal Jesus to our hearts. Oh, Holy Spirit, do this for Begum Sheikh. Amen."

We stayed on our knees for what seemed like forever. I was glad for the silence, for my heart was strangely warmed.

At last Mrs. Mitchell and I arose. "Is that a Bible, Madame Sheikh?" she asked, nodding toward the little gray volume which I clutched to my breast in one hand. I showed her the book. "How do you find it?" she asked. "Easy to understand?"

"Not really," I said. "It is an old translation and I'm not at home in it."

She stepped into an adjacent room and returned with another book.

"Here is a New Testament written in modern English," she said. "It's called the Phillips translation. I find it much easier to understand than others. Would you like it?"

"Yes," I said, not hesitating.

"Start with the Gospel of John," Mrs. Mitchell advised, opening the book and placing a bit of paper in it as a bookmark. "That's another John, but he makes the role of John the Baptist very clear."

"Thank you," I said, touched. "And now I think I've taken too much of your time."

As I prepared to leave, Mrs. Mitchell said: "You know, it's so interesting that a dream brought you here. God often speaks to His children in dreams and visions."

As she helped me on with my coat, I wondered if I should share something about my other dream with her. The one about the perfume salesman. It seemed so . . . bizarre. But as had happened several times already in this strange evening, I found myself filled with a boldness that seemed almost to come from outside of me. "Mrs. Mitchell, can you tell me if there is a connection between perfume and Jesus?"

She thought for a moment, her hand on the door. "No," she said, "I can't think of any. However, let me pray about it."

As I drove home, I experienced for the second time that same fragrant Presence I had sensed in my garden earlier that day!

When I got home that night I read a little out of the portion of the Bible called "The Gospel of John," where the writer talked about John the Baptist, this strange man clad in camel skin who came out of the wilderness, calling people to prepare for the coming of the Lord. And then, there in the safety of my own bedroom, seated on my divan, surrounded by memories and traditions that were seven centuries old, a thought slipped sideways into my mind, unbidden, unwanted, quickly rejected. If John the Baptist was a sign from God, a sign pointing toward Jesus, was this same man pointing *me* toward Jesus, too?

Of course the thought was untenable. I put it out of mind and went to sleep.

That night I did sleep soundly.

As the muezzin called me to prayer the next morning, I was relieved to find myself seeing things clearly again. What a bizarre series of thoughts I had toyed with in the night! But now as the muezzin reminded me where truth lay, I felt secure again, away from these disturbing Christian influences.

Raisham came in just then, not with tea but with a note which she said had just been delivered to the house.

It was from Mrs. Mitchell. All it said was: "Read Second Corinthians, Chapter 2, Verse 14."

I reached for the Bible she had given me and searched until I found the chapter and verse. Then, as I read, I caught my breath:

> *Thanks be to God who leads us, wherever we are, on Christ's triumphant way, and makes our knowledge of Him spread throughout the world like a lovely perfume!*

I sat there in bed, and re-read the passage, my composure of a minute ago shattered. The knowledge of Jesus spreads like a lovely perfume! In my dream, the salesman had put the golden dish of scent on my bedside table and said that the perfume "would spread throughout the world." The next morning I had found my Bible in the same spot where the perfume had been laid! It was all too clear. I didn't want to think about it any more. Ring for tea, that's what I must do. Ring for my tea and bring life back into its proper focus quickly before something else went awry.

Even though Mrs. Mitchell had invited me back, I felt it best not to return. It seemed a prudent logical decision that I must now investigate this Bible on my own. I did not want to be pushed by any outside influence. However, one afternoon Nur-jan rushed into my room with an odd look in her eyes. "The Reverend and Mrs. Mitchell are here to see you," she gasped.

My hand flew to my throat. Why would they come *here?* I wondered. However, quickly composing myself, I asked the maid to bring them into the drawing room.

Sandy-haired David Mitchell, a lanky man with crinkly eyes, radiated the same friendly warmth as his wife. The two seemed so happy to see me that I forgot my discomfort over them coming to my house.

Mrs. Mitchell started to shake hands, then at the last minute threw her arms around me instead. I was stunned. No one outside the family, not even our closest friends, had ever embraced me in this way before. I stiffened but Mrs. Mitchell appeared to take no notice of my reaction. I found —in retrospect, I have to admit—that this display pleased me. There could have been no sham in her greeting.

"I'm so happy to meet 'the Flower Lady'," David exclaimed in a jovial American accent.

I glanced at Mrs. Mitchell and she laughed. "I should explain. When you came to our house, I wanted to let David know right away by telegram for we had often talked about you since we visited your garden last spring. However, I didn't want to use your real name, to protect you. As I was wondering how to refer to you in the wire, I glanced out my window and saw the flowers that had grown from the seeds your gardener gave us. The name came to me: 'Flower Lady,' and that became our code name for you."

I laughed. "Well, from now on, you can call me Bilquis."

"And please," she said, "call me Synnove."

It was a strange visit. I suppose I was half expecting pressure from the Mitchells to accept their religion, but nothing of the sort occurred. We drank a cup of tea and chatted. I did question Jesus being called the "son of God," for to Muslims there is no greater sin than to make this claim. The Koran states again and again that God has no children. "And this 'trinity'?" I asked. "God is three?"

In answer, David compared God to the sun which manifests itself in the three creative energies of heat, light and radiation, a trinity relationship which together makes the sun, yet singly is not the sun. And then shortly they left.

Again for several days I found myself alone with two books—the Koran and the Bible. I continued to read them both, studying the Koran because of the loyalty of a lifetime, delving into the Bible because of a strange inner hunger.

Yet, sometimes I'd draw back from picking up the Bible. God couldn't be in both books, I knew, because their messages were so different. But when my hand hesitated at picking up the book Mrs. Mitchell gave me, I felt a strange

letdown. For the past week I had been living in a world of
beauty, not a visible garden created by me from seeds and
water, but an inner garden created from a new spiritual
awareness. I first entered this world of beauty by way of
my two dreams; then I became aware of this world a second
time on the night I met the indefinably glorious Presence in
my garden; and I had known it once again when I obeyed
the nudging that prompted me to visit the Mitchells.

Slowly, clearly, over the next few days I began to know
that there was a way to return to my world of beauty.
And reading this Christian book seemed, for reasons that
I could not grasp, the key to my re-entering that world.

And then one day little Mahmud came up to me holding
the side of his head and trying not to whimper. "My ear,
Mum," he cried in a pain-filled voice. "It hurts."

I bent down and examined him carefully. His usual ruddy
brown complexion had paled, and although Mahmud was
not a child to complain, I could see the tear stains on his
little round tan cheeks.

I put him right to bed and crooned softly to him, his
black hair too stark against the pillow. And then, after his
eyes closed, I went to the telephone and rang the Holy
Family Hospital in Rawalpindi. Within a minute Tooni
was on the phone. She agreed that we should check Mahmud
into the hospital the next afternoon for a complete examina-
tion the following day. I would be able to stay in an adjoining room and a maid would be given a smaller room
adjacent to that.

It was toward evening when we checked into the comfortable arrangement. Tooni had the evening free to spend
with us. Soon, Mahmud and his mother were giggling over
some pictures Mahmud was coloring in a book she had
brought him. I was propped up in bed reading my Bible.
I had also brought the Koran with me, but by now I read
the Koran out of a sense of duty, more than interest.

Suddenly, the room lights flickered, and then went out.
The room was dark.

"Another power failure," I said, exasperated. "Did you see any candles?"

In a moment the door opened and a nun stepped inside with a flashlight. "I hope you don't mind the dark," she said cheerily. "We'll get some candles shortly." I recognized her as Dr. Pia Santiago, a slightly built, bespectacled Filipino who was in charge of the whole hospital. We had met briefly on a previous visit. Almost at once another nun came in with candles and in a moment warm light flooded the room. Mahmud and Tooni resumed their visit and I was left to make conversation with Dr. Santiago. I couldn't help notice her staring at my Bible.

"Do you mind if I sit with you for a while?" Dr. Santiago asked.

"It would be a pleasure," I said, assuming it was just a courtesy visit. She moved to a chair near my bed and with a rustling of her white habit sat down.

"Oh," she said, taking off her glasses and wiping her brow with a handkerchief, "has this ever been a busy night."

My heart warmed to her. Muslims always had respect for these holy women who give up the world to serve their God; their faith may be misplaced, but their sincerity was real. We chatted but as the conversation continued, I could tell that this woman had something on her mind. It was the Bible. I could see her glancing at it with mounting curiosity. Finally she leaned forward and in a confidential tone asked, "Madame Sheikh, what are you doing with a Bible?"

"I am earnestly in search of God," I answered. And then, while the candles burned lower, I told her, very cautiously at first, then with mounting boldness, about my dreams, my visit with Mrs. Mitchell, and my comparing the Bible and the Koran. "Whatever happens," I emphasized, "I must find God, but I'm confused about your faith," I said finally, realizing that even as I spoke I was putting my finger on something important. "You seem to make God so . . . I don't know . . . *personal!*"

The little nun's eyes filled with compassion and she leaned forward. "Madame Sheikh," she said, her voice full of emotion, "there is only one way to find out why we feel this way. And that is to find out for yourself, strange as that may seem. Why don't you pray *to* the God you are searching for? Ask Him to show you His way. Talk to Him as if He were your friend."

I smiled. She might as well suggest that I talk to the Taj Mahal. But then Dr. Santiago said something that shot through my being like electricity. She leaned closer and took my hand in hers, tears streaming down her cheeks. "Talk to Him," she said very quietly, "as if He were your father."

I sat back quickly. A dead silence filled the room. Even Mahmud and Tooni's conversation hung between thoughts. I stared at the nun with the candlelight glinting off her glasses.

Talk to God as if He were my father! The thought shook my soul in the peculiar way truth has of being at once startling and comforting.

Then as if on cue everyone started talking at once. Tooni and Mahmud laughed and decided that the parasol should be colored purple. Dr. Santiago smiled, rose, wished us all well, gathered her habit about her and left the room.

Nothing else was said about prayer or Christianity. Yet I moved through the rest of that night, and the next morning, stunned. What made the experience especially mysterious was that the doctors could find nothing wrong with Mahmud and Mahmud kept saying that his ear did not hurt him one bit. At first, I was irritated at all the time and trouble this had taken. Then the thought occurred to me that perhaps, just perhaps, in some mystic way God had taken advantage of this situation to bring me into contact with Dr. Santiago.

Later that morning Manzur drove us all back to Wah. As we turned off the Grand Trunk onto our lane, I could see the gray roof of my home through the trees. Usually, I looked forward to home as a retreat from the world. But today there seemed to be a difference about my house, as if something special would happen to me there.

We drove up the long driveway, Manzur sounding the horn. The servants ran out and surrounded the car. "Is the little one well?" they all asked at once.

Yes, I assured them, Mahmud was fine. But my mind was not on homecoming festivities. It was on this new way to find God. I went up to my bedroom to consider all that had been happening. No Muslim, I felt certain, ever thought of Allah as his father. Since childhood, I had been told that the surest way to know about Allah was to pray five times a day and study and think on the Koran. Yet Dr. Santiago's words came to me again. "Talk *to* God. Talk to Him as if He were your Father."

Alone in my room I got on my knees and tried to call Him "Father." But it was a useless effort and I straightened in dismay. It was ridiculous. Wouldn't it be sinful to try to bring the Great One down to our own level? I fell asleep that night more confused than ever.

Hours later I awoke. It was after midnight, my birthday, December 12th. I was 47 years old. I felt a momentary excitement, a carry-over from childhood when birthdays were festivals with string bands on the lawns, games, and relatives coming to the house all day. Now, there would be no celebration, perhaps a few phone calls, nothing more.

Oh, how I had missed those childhood days. I thought of my parents as I liked to remember them best. Mother, so loving, so regal and beautiful. And Father. I had been so proud of him, with his high posts in the Indian government. I could still see him, impeccably dressed, adjusting his turban at the mirror before leaving for his office. The friendly eyes under bushy brows, the gentle smile, the chiseled features and aquiline nose.

One of my cherished memories was seeing him at work in the study. Even in a society where sons were more highly regarded than daughters, Father prized his children equally. Often, as a little girl, I would have a question to ask him and I would peek at him from around the door of his office, hesitant to interrupt. Then his eye would catch mine. Putting down his pen, he would lean back in his chair and call out, "Keecha?" Slowly, I would walk into the study, my head down. He would smile and pat the chair next to his. "Come, my darling, sit here." Then, placing his arm around me, he would draw me to him. "Now, my little Keecha," he would ask gently, "What can I do for you?"

It was always the same with Father. He didn't mind if I bothered him. Whenever I had a question or problem, no matter how busy he was, he would put aside his work to devote his full attention just to me.

It was well past midnight as I lay in bed savoring this wonderful memory. "Oh thank you . . ." I murmured to God. Was I really talking *to* Him?

Suddenly, a breakthrough of hope flooded me. Suppose, just suppose God were like a father. If my earthly father would put aside everything to listen to me, wouldn't my heavenly Father . . . ?

Shaking with excitement, I got out of bed, sank to my knees on the rug, looked up to heaven and in rich new understanding called God "My Father."

I was not prepared for what happened.

5.

The Crossroads

"Oh Father, my Father . . . Father God."

Hesitantly, I spoke His name aloud. I tried different ways of speaking to Him. And then, as if something broke through for me I found myself trusting that He was indeed hearing me, just as my earthly father had always done.

"Father, oh my Father God," I cried, with growing confidence. My voice seemed unusually loud in the large bedroom as I knelt on the rug beside my bed. But suddenly that room wasn't empty any more. *He* was there! I could sense His Presence. I could feel His hand laid gently on my head. It was as if I could *see* His eyes, filled with love and compassion. He was so close that I found myself laying my head on His knees like a little girl sitting at her father's feet. For a long time I knelt there, sobbing quietly, floating in His love. I found myself talking with Him, apologizing for not having known Him before. And again, came His loving compassion, like a warm blanket settling around me.

Now I recognized this as the same loving Presence I had met that fragrance-filled afternoon in my garden. The same Presence I had sensed often as I read the Bible.

"I am confused, Father . . ." I said. "I have to get one thing straight right away." I reached over to the bedside table where I kept the Bible and the Koran side by side.

I picked up both books and lifted them, one in each hand. "Which, Father?" I said. "Which one is Your book?"

Then a remarkable thing happened. Nothing like it had ever occurred in my life in quite this way. For I heard a voice inside my being, a voice that spoke to me as clearly as if I were repeating words in my inner mind. They were fresh, full of kindness, yet at the same time full of authority.

"In which book do you meet Me as your Father?"

I found myself answering: "In the Bible." That's all it took. Now there was no question in my mind which one was His book. I looked at my watch and was astonished to discover that three hours had passed. Yet I was not tired. I wanted to go on praying, I wanted to read the Bible, for I knew now that my Father would speak through it. I went to bed only when I knew I must for the sake of my health. But the very next morning I told my maids to see that I was not disturbed, took my Bible again and reclined on my divan. Starting with Matthew, I began reading the New Testament word by word.

I was impressed that God spoke to His people in dreams, five times in the first part of Matthew, in fact! He spoke to Joseph on behalf of Mary. He warned the Wise Men about Herod, and three more times He addressed Joseph concerning the protection of the baby Jesus.

I couldn't find enough time for the Bible. Everything I read, it seemed, was directing me to take some kind of closer walk with God.

I found myself standing at a great crossroads. So far I had met, personally, the Father God. In my heart I knew I had to give myself totally to His Son Jesus or else to turn my back on Him completely.

And I knew for certain that everyone I loved would advise me to turn my back on Jesus. Into my mind crowded the memory of a special, precious day years before when my father took me to our family mosque, just the two of us. We stepped into the soaring vaulted chamber. Taking my hand, Father told me with great pride and with strong identification that twenty generations of our family had worshipped there. "What a privilege you have, my little Keecha, to be part of this ancient truth."

And I thought of Tooni. Surely this young woman had enough worries already. And there were my other children; although they lived far away, they too would be hurt if I "became a Christian." And then there was my Uncle Fateh, who had watched so proudly the day I was four years, four months, four days old and began learning to read the Koran. And there was beloved Aunt Amina and all my other relatives, some hundred "uncles," "aunts" and "cousins." In the east, the family becomes *biraderi*, one community, with each member responsible to the other. I could hurt the family in many ways, even interfere with the opportunities of my nieces getting married, as they would have to live in the shadow of my decision if I chose to join the "sweepers."

But most of all I worried about my little grandson, Mahmud; what would happen to him! My heart caught at the thought of Mahmud's father. He was a very volatile man, who might easily try to take the boy from me if I became a Christian, therefore clearly demonstrating that I was unstable.

That day as I sat reading and thinking in my quiet room, these thoughts seared my heart. Suddenly, the realization of the pain I might inflict on others became too much for me and I stood up, crying. I threw a wrap around me and walked into the cold, winter garden, my refuge where, it seemed, I could think best.

"Oh Lord," I cried, as I paced the graveled path, "could You really want me to leave my family? Can a God of love want me to inflict pain on others?" And in the darkness of my despair, all I could hear were His words, the words which I had just read in Matthew:

Anyone who puts his love for father or mother above his love for me does not deserve to be mine, and he

*who loves son or daughter more than me is not worthy
of me. . . .*

Matthew 10:37–38

This Jesus did not compromise. He did not want any
competition. His were hard, uncomfortable words, words I
did not want to hear.

Enough! I couldn't take the pressure of the decision any
longer. On impulse I ran back to the house, summoned
Manzur and announced to the somewhat startled housekeeper that I was going to Rawalpindi. I would be gone
for a few days. She could reach me at my daughter's if there
were need. Manzur drove me into Rawalpindi where I did
spend several days feverishly shopping, buying toys for
Mahmud, perfumes and saris for myself. Not surprisingly,
as I continued my spree, I found myself drifting away from
the warmth of His Presence. Once when a shopkeeper
spread out a piece of cloth and showed me the gems em-
broidered in a rich design, I suddenly saw the shape of the
cross in the pattern. I snapped at the shopkeeper and fled.
The next morning I went back to Wah neither determined
to remain a Muslim nor determined to become a Christian.

Then one evening as I relaxed before the fire, I found
myself picking up the Bible again. Mahmud was in bed.
It was quiet in the living room. A wind in the garden rattled
the windows, the fire snapped and hissed.

I had read straight through all the Gospels and the Book
of Acts, and that night I had reached the last book in the
Bible. I was fascinated by Revelation, even though I understood very little of it. I read as if directed, strangely confident. And then abruptly I came to a sentence that made
the room spin. It was the 20th verse of the third chapter of
Revelation:

*See, I stand knocking at the door. If anyone listens to
my voice and opens the door, I will go into his house
and dine with him, and he with me.*

And dine with Him, and He with me!

I gasped, letting the book fall in my lap.

This was my dream, the dream where Jesus was having dinner with me! At the time I had had no knowledge of a book called Revelation. I closed my eyes and once again I could see Jesus sitting across the table from me. I could feel His warm smile, His acceptance. Why, the glory was there too! Just as it had been with the Father. It was the glory that belonged to His Presence!

Now I knew that my dream had come from God. The way was clear. I could accept Him, or reject Him. I could open the door, ask Him to come in permanently, or I could close the door. I would have to make my full decision *now*, one way or the other.

I made up my mind and knelt in front of the fire.

"Oh God, don't wait a moment. Please come into my life. Every bit of me is open to You." I did not have to struggle, or worry about what would happen. I had said Yes. Christ was in my life now, and I knew it.

How unbearably beautiful. Within a few days I had met God the Father and God the Son. I got up and started to prepare for bed, my mind whirling. Did I dare take one more step? I remembered that in the book of Acts, at Pentecost, Jesus had baptized His followers with the Holy Spirit. Was I supposed to follow this same pattern? "Lord," I said, as I laid my head back on my pillow, "I have no one to guide me except You Yourself. If You intend for me to receive this Baptism in the Holy Spirit then of course I want what You want. I am ready." Knowing I had placed myself completely in His hands, I drifted off to sleep.

It was still dark when I was awakened in a state of vibrant expectancy that morning of December 24, 1966. I looked at my luminescent clock and the hands pointed to 3:00 A.M. The room was bitterly cold but I was burning with excitement.

I crawled out of bed and sank to my knees on the cold rug. As I looked up, I seemed to be looking into a great light. Hot tears flowed down my face as I raised my hands to Him and cried out: "Oh Father God, baptize me with Your Holy Spirit!"

I took my Bible and opened it to where the Lord said:

John used to baptize with water, but before many days are passed you will be baptized with the Holy Spirit.
                                                    Acts 1:5

"Lord," I cried, "if these words of Yours are true, then give this baptism to me now." I crumpled face down on the chilled floor where I lay crying. "Lord," I sobbed, "I'll never want to get up from this place until You give me this baptism." Suddenly, I was filled with wonder and awe. For in that silent pre-dawn room I saw His face. Something surged through me, wave after wave of purifying ocean breakers, flooding me to the tips of my fingers and toes, washing my soul.

Then the powerful surges subsided, the heavenly ocean quieted. I was completely cleansed. Joy exploded within me and I cried out praising Him, thanking Him.

Hours later, I felt the Lord lift me to my feet. He wanted me to get up now. I looked out the filigreed windows and saw that it was nearly dawn.

"Oh, Lord," I said, as I lay back in my bed. "Could the heaven you speak of be any better than this? To know You is joy, to worship You is happiness, to be near You is peace. *This* is heaven!"

I doubt if I slept two hours that early dawn. In no time at all my maidservants came in to help me dress. For the first morning that I could remember, I did not say one cross word to them. Instead there was an air of calm and peace in the sun-flooded room. Raisham actually hummed a song as she brushed my hair, something she had never done before.

All that day I roamed through my house, silently praising God, hardly able to contain the joy within myself. At lunch,

Mahmud looked up from his pancakes and said: "Mum, you look so smiley; what has happened to you?"

I reached over and tousled his shiny black hair. "Give him some *halwa*," I told the cook. This dish made from wheat, butter and sugar was his favorite sweet. I told Mahmud that we would be celebrating Christmas at the Mitchells' home.

"Christmas?" said Mahmud.

"It's a holiday," I said, "a little like Ramazan." That, Mahmud did understand. Ramazan was the month of the Muslim year when Muhammad received his first revelation. So for this month, each year, Muslims fast from sunrise to sunset each day until at last the drums thunder in the mosques and we load ourselves with delicacies, sweet and sour fruit, spinach leaves dipped in batter and fried, delicately cooked eggplant, succulent kabobs. Christmas I supposed would indeed be a little like Ramazan. And I was right. When David met us at the door of the Mitchells' house, the scent of delicious cooked foods floated around him, and laughter sounded from within the room.

"Come in! Come in!" he exclaimed, drawing us into the living room filled with a holiday spirit. A Christmas tree glowed in the corner and the laughter of the two Mitchell children, just a little older than Mahmud, rang out from another room. Mahmud happily joined them at their play.

I could not contain my joy any longer. "David!" I cried, using his first name without thinking, "I am a Christian now! I have been baptized in the Holy Spirit!"

He stared at me for a moment, then drew me into the house. "Who told you about the Holy Spirit Baptism?" he asked, his gray eyes wide. He began laughing joyously and praising God. Hearing his "Hallelujah!" Synnove rushed into the room from the kitchen and David again asked: "Who told you?"

"Jesus told me," I laughed. "I read it in the Bible's Book of Acts; I asked God for it and received it."

Both David and Synnove looked bewildered. But then

suddenly they rushed to me. Synnove put her arms around me and broke into tears. David joined her. Then the three of us stood there, arms around each other, praising God for what He had done.

That night I began a diary into which I put all the wonderful things the Lord had been doing for me. If I should die—and I had no idea what might happen to me once word got out that I had become a Christian—at least I wanted this record of my experience to remain. As I sat at my desk writing my experiences, I did not realize that He was making preparations to begin my education.

6.

Learning to Find His Presence

Several surprises were waiting for me over the next several days, following my threefold encounters.

For one thing, I found I was experiencing dreams or visions, but quite unlike the two dreams that had started this whole incredible adventure. In fact my first experience left me shaken. I was resting in bed one afternoon thinking of my Lord when suddenly I felt as if I were floating right out my window. I felt sure I was not asleep and found myself passing right through the window filigree, and I caught a glimpse of the earth below. I became so frightened that I cried out in fear, and suddenly I found myself back in bed. I lay there slightly dazed, breathing shallowly, feeling a tingling in my legs as if they had been asleep, and then the blood was rushing back.

"What was it, Lord?" I asked. And then I realized that He had given me a special experience. "I'm so sorry, Lord," I apologized, "but You have picked up a coward."

Late that night it happened again. Only this time I talked to God through the experience and told Him I wasn't afraid. As I slipped back through my window I could only think I had been "floating" in a spiritual way. "But what is Your reason, my Lord?" I asked.

Turning to the Bible I searched His Word for something

of this, for I began to fear that it might be something not of the Lord.

I sighed in relief when I read in the Acts of the Apostles (8:39) where the Spirit of the Lord suddenly whisked Philip away to the distant city of Azotus after he had baptized the Ethiopian eunuch.

Then I was given further confirmation when I read Paul's second letter to the Christians at Corinth. In chapter 12, in speaking of visions and revelations from the Lord, he wrote of being "caught up into the third heaven." He felt that only God knew whether or not it was an actual physical experience, and I felt the same about mine. As Paul added: "This man heard words that cannot . . . be translated into human speech."

I heard words, too, that I cannot translate but I shall never forget the scenes. During one such experience I saw a steeple soaring into heaven; suddenly before me were hundreds of churches, new ones, old ones, churches with different architectural styles, and then a beautiful gold church. Again the scene shifted and I saw downtown areas of cities rolling before me, modern centers and old-fashioned village squares. It was all so clear; I could discern the skyscrapers, clock towers, and quaint ornate buildings.

Then my heart shook as I saw a man riding a red horse, his right hand wielding a sword; he galloped about the earth under cloud masses. Sometimes he rose until his head touched the clouds, and sometimes his steed's flashing hooves scraped the earth.

I couldn't get over the feeling that these must have been given to me for a particular, still unknown, reason.

I also found as I read the Scriptures that it was an experience completely unlike any other time I had spent with the Bible. Something happened to me as I went through the book; instead of reading the Bible, I found myself living it. It was as if I stepped through its pages into that ancient world of Palestine when Jesus Christ walked the stony roads of Galilee. I watched as He preached and taught, as He lived out His message in everyday situations, and as He displayed the power of the Spirit, and finally as He went to the cross and passed victoriously through the experience of death.

I also discovered to my surprise that the effect of Bible reading was beginning to be felt by others. This was brought home to me one morning when my maids were preparing my toilette. Nur-jan was arranging the silver combs and brushes on a tray when she accidently spilled the whole thing. There was a great clatter. She stiffened, her eyes wide; I knew she was expecting my usual onslaught. And indeed I was about to scold her when I caught myself. Instead, I found myself saying, "Don't worry, Nur-jan. They didn't break."

Then there was a peculiar boldness that began to take shape in my life. Up until then I had been afraid to let anyone know of my interest in Christ. For one thing, I dreaded the thought of people making jokes about the "sweeper Begum." Of more concern, I was afraid my family would ostracize me; Mahmud's father might even try to take him away. I was even fearful lest some fanatic take to heart the injunction: *he who falls away from his faith must die.*

So I was really not anxious to be seen at the Mitchells. The group of women who came out of David's and Synnove's house that first night still gave me concern. My own servants certainly knew that something unusual was happening to me. When I put all this together I was living in a state of constant uneasiness, not knowing when the pressure against me would begin.

But after my three encounters with God, I found myself making a surprising admission to myself one day. As far as I was concerned, my decision to become a Christian was now public information. As the Bible says, I was "confessing Jesus with my lips." "Well," I said to myself as I stood at my bedroom window one day, "we'll just let the results fall where they may."

I didn't expect results quite so quickly. Soon after Christmas, 1966, the downstairs maid came to me with her eyebrows arched, "Mrs. Mitchell is here to see you, Begum," she said.

"Oh?" I said, trying to sound casual, "show her in." My heart pounded as I walked to the door to meet my guest. "I am so honored to have you visit," I said, making sure that the maid, hovering in the background, heard me.

Synnove came to invite me to dinner. "There will be a few others there, people we are sure you would like to meet," she said.

Others? I felt the old wall rise within me. Synnove must have caught the hesitant look in my eyes for she sought to reassure me. "Most of them are Christians," she said. "Some are English, some Americans. Would you come?" her eyes pleaded hopefully.

And of course—with more enthusiasm than I felt—I said that I would be delighted.

I wondered why many Christians were so often shy! I had been in contact with Christians before, usually at state dinner parties I had hosted as wife of a government official. The dinners were formal events, served by uniformed servants, amidst Belgian lace, with centerpieces of fresh flowers; lengthy affairs, with numerous courses each served separately on its own Spode china. There were many Christians of different nationalities among the guests, but not one of them ever mentioned his faith, even when it would have been a natural part of the conversation. The people I'd meet at the Mitchell's, I felt, would not be so backward.

The next day I drove the now becoming familiar route to the Mitchells' house. David and Synnove greeted me warmly and introduced me to their friends. I wonder how I would have felt if I'd known at the time how large a role some of these people were going to play in my life.

The first couple were Ken and Marie Old. Ken was an Englishman whose blue eyes twinkled humorously behind thick glasses. He was a civil engineer who wore an air of informality as easily as he wore his rumpled clothes. His wife Marie was an American nurse with a practical air offset by a beautiful smile. The others were warm and friendly people, too.

And then to my horror I found myself the center of attention. Everyone was eager to hear about my experiences. What I expected to be a quiet dinner turned out to be a question and answer period. The dining room was still—even the several children sat quietly—as I told about my dreams, and about my separate meetings with the three personalities of God. At the end of the dinner David complimented his wife on the meal but said he felt that the spiritual nourishment of my story was even richer.

"I agree," said Ken Old. "I've seen you before, you know. I used to live in Wah. I would pass your garden in the early morning and admire your flowers. Sometimes you were in the garden but I must say you don't look like the same woman." I felt sure I knew what he meant. The Bilquis Sheikh of a few months ago had been an unsmiling person. "You are like a child," Ken went on to say, "who has suddenly been given a gift. In your face I see an incredible wonder at that gift. You treasure it more than anything you have ever possessed."

I was going to like this man.

I had enjoyable conversations with the others, and I realized that I had been right. These Christians were very different from Christians I had met at other dinner parties. Before the evening was over, each person had told a little about what the Lord was doing in his life. David was right. The meal was excellent, but the true feeding came from the Presence in that little house. I had never known anything similar, and I found myself wishing I could get this same feeding regularly.

Which is why, as I was about to leave, the comment from Ken struck me with such impact. Ken and Marie came up and took my hand. "You'll need some regular Christian fellowship now, Bilquis," said Ken. "Will you come to our house on Sunday evenings."

"Could you?" asked Marie hopefully.

And that is how I began regular meetings with other Christians. Sunday evenings we met at the Olds' house, a brick dwelling whose living room could barely hold the dozen people who crowded in. Only two were Pakistanis, the rest were Americans and Englishmen. I met new people, too, such as Dr. and Mrs. Christy. This thin energetic-looking American doctor was an eye specialist and his wife a nurse. Both were on the local mission hospital staff. At the meetings we sang, read the Bible, and prayed for each other's needs. It quickly became the high point of my week.

Then one Sunday I didn't particularly feel like going. So I rang up the Olds and gave some excuse. It seemed a little thing, but almost instantly I began to feel uneasy. What was it! I walked through the house restlessly checking on the servants' work. Everything was in order, yet everything seemed out of order.

Then I went to my own room and knelt down to pray. After a while Mahmud crept in, so quietly that I didn't know he was there until I felt his little soft hand in mine. "Mum, are you all right?" he asked. "You look funny." I smiled and assured him that, yes, I was all right. "Well you keep walking around *looking*. As if you'd lost something."

Then he was gone, skipping out the door and down the hall. I looked as if I had lost something?! Mahmud was right. And I knew right then what it was I had lost. I'd lost the sense of God's glory. It was gone! Why? Did it have something to do with my not going to that meeting at the Olds'? With my not having fellowship when I needed it?

With a sense of urgency I phoned Ken and said that I'd be there after all.

What a difference. Immediately I felt, actually felt, the return of warmth to my soul. I did go to the meeting, as I promised. Nothing unusual took place there, yet again I knew I was walking in His glory. Ken had apparently been right. I *needed* fellowship. I had learned my lesson. I determined from then on to attend regularly unless Jesus Himself told me not to go.

As I drew a little closer to God, here a step, there a step, I found myself hungering even more for His word through the Bible. Everyday, as soon as I arose, I would begin reading it with a never-failing sense of *nowness*. The Bible became alive to me, illuminating my day, shedding its light on every step I would take. It was, in fact, my lovely perfume. But here too I found a strange thing. One day Mahmud and I were to go to see his mother for the day. I was late getting to bed the night before and really didn't feel like getting up at dawn to have an hour with the Bible, so I told Raisham to wake me with my tea just before we were supposed to set off.

I didn't sleep at all well that night. I tossed and twisted and had bad dreams. When Raisham came in, I was exhausted. And I noticed that the entire day didn't go right.

Strange! What was the Lord saying to me? That He expected me to read the Bible *every* day?

That was the second time when I seemed to be stepping out of the glory of the Lord's Presence.

But the experience, nonetheless, left me with a strange sense of excitement. For I had the feeling that I was sitting on an important truth without realizing it. There were times when I was in the Presence and experienced that deep sense of joy and peace, and there were times when I lost the sense of His Presence.

What was the key? What could I do to stay close to Him?

I thought back over the times when He had seemed unusually close, way back to my two dreams and to the afternoon when I sensed the exquisite fragrance in my winter garden. I thought about the first time when I had gone to the Mitchells' and about the later times when I had read my Bible regularly, and gone to the Sunday meetings at the Olds'. Almost always these were times when I knew the Lord was with me.

And I thought about opposite times too, moments when I knew that I had lost this sense of His nearness. How did the Bible put it? *And grieve not the Holy Spirit of God* (Ephesians 4:30, KJV). Is that what happened when I scolded the servants? Or when I failed to nourish my spirit with regular Bible reading? Or when I just didn't go to the Olds'?

Part of the key to staying in His company was obedience. When I obeyed, then I was allowed to remain in His Presence.

I got out my Bible and searched in John until I found the verse where Jesus says:

> *When a man loves me, he follows my teaching. Then my Father will love him, and we will come to that man and make our home within him.*
>
> John 14:23

That was the Bible's way of expressing what I was trying to say. To stay in the glory. *That* was what I was trying to do!

And the key was obedience. "Oh Father," I prayed, "I want to be Your servant, just as it says in the Bible. I *will* obey You. I've always thought it a sacrifice to give up my own will. But it's no sacrifice because it keeps me close to You. How could Your Presence be a sacrifice!"

I had never got used to those times when the Lord seemed to speak so directly to my mind, as I am convinced He did right then. Who else but the Lord would have asked me to forgive my husband! *Love your former husband, Bilquis. Forgive him.*

For a moment I sat in shock. Feeling His love for people in general was one thing, but to love this man who had hurt me so much?

"Father, I just can't do it. I don't want to bless Khalid or forgive him." I recalled how once I had childishly even asked the Lord not ever to convert my husband because then he would have the same joy that I had. And now God was asking me to *love* this same man? I could feel anger rising within me as I thought of Khalid, and quickly put him out of my mind. "Maybe I could just forget him, Lord. Wouldn't that be enough?"

Was it my imagination or did the glow of the Lord's Presence seem to cool? "I can't forgive my husband, Lord. I have no capacity to do so."

My yoke is easy and my burden is light (Matthew 11:30).

"Lord, I can't forgive him!" I cried. Then I listed all the terrible things he had done to me. As I did, other wounds surfaced, hurts that I had pushed into the back of my mind as too humiliating to think about. Hate welled within me and now I felt totally separated from God. Frightened, I cried out like a lost child.

And quickly, miraculously, He was there, with me in my room. Flinging myself at His feet, I confessed my hate and my inability to forgive.

My yoke is easy and my burden is light.

Slowly, deliberately, I swung my terrible burden over to Him. I let go of my resentment, my hurt, and the festering outrage, placing it all in His hands. Suddenly I sensed a light rising within me, like the glow of dawn. Breathing freely, I hurried to my dresser and took out the gold-framed picture and looked down at Khalid's face. I prayed: "Oh Father, take away my resentment and fill me with Your love for Khalid in the name of my Lord and Savior, Jesus Christ."

I stood there for a long time, looking at the picture. Slowly the negative feeling within me began to fade. In its place came an unexpected love, a sense of caring for the man in the photo. I couldn't believe it. I was actually wishing my former husband well.

"Oh bless him, Lord, give him joy, let him be happy in his new life."

As I willed this, a dark cloud lifted from me. A weight was removed from my soul. I felt peaceful, relaxed.

Once again I found myself living in His glory.

And once again I found myself wanting never to leave His company. As a reminder to myself of this desire, I went downstairs, late as it was, and found some henna dye. With it I drew a large cross on the back of both hands to remind me always.

Never, if I had anything to say about it, would I again deliberately step away from His company.

It would take me a long time, I was sure, to learn the skill of living in the glow of His Presence, but it was a training time I welcomed with immense excitement.

And then one night I had a terrifying experience. I did not know I would be hearing from another side.

7.

The Baptism of Fire and Water

I had been sound asleep that night in January 1967 when I was startled awake by my bed shaking violently.

An earthquake? My heart was gripped by a nameless terror. And then I sensed a horrible malevolent presence in my room; one that was definitely evil.

Suddenly I was thrown out of my bed; whether I was in my physical body or spirit I do not know. But I was pushed and thrown about like a straw in a hurricane. The face of Mahmud flashed before me and my heart cried out for his protection.

This must be death coming for me, I thought, my soul quaking. The awful presence engulfed me like a black billowing cloud and instinctively I screamed out to the One Who now meant everything to me. "Oh Lord Jesus!" At this I was shaken mightily, as a dog ravages his prey.

"Am I wrong to call on Jesus?" I cried to God in my spirit. At this a great strength surged through me and I called out: "I *will* call on Him! Jesus! Jesus! Jesus!"

At this the powerful ravaging subsided. I lay there worshipping and praising the Lord. However, sometime around 3:00 in the morning, my eyelids became too heavy and I slipped to sleep.

I was awakened in the morning by Raisham bringing me

my morning tea. I lay there for a moment feeling such a sense of relief. As I closed my eyes in prayer, I saw the Lord Jesus Christ standing before me. He wore a white robe and a purple cape. He gently smiled at me and said, "Don't worry; it won't happen again."

I felt then that my harrowing experience was Satanic, a test Jesus permitted for my own good. I recalled the cry that came from deep within my soul: "I *will* call on His Name, I *will* say Jesus Christ."

My Lord was still standing before me. *It is time for you to be baptized in water, Bilquis,* He said.

Water baptism! I had heard the words distinctly, and I didn't like what I heard.

As soon as I could I dressed and asked Nur-jan and Raisham to see that I wasn't disturbed until lunchtime. I stood at the window thinking. The morning air was cool; and pale steam drifted up from the garden springs. I knew that the significance of baptism is not lost on the Muslim world. A person can read the Bible without arousing too much hostility. But the sacrament of baptism is a different matter. To the Muslim this is the one unmistakable sign that a convert has renounced his Islamic faith to become a Christian. To the Muslim, baptism is apostasy.

So, here was a difficult testing point. The issue was clearly drawn. Would I yield to the fear of being treated as an outcast, or worse, as a traitor, or would I obey Jesus?

First of all I had to be certain that I was really obeying the Lord, and not some illusion. For I was far too new at being a Christian to trust "voices." How could I test my impression better than through the Bible. So I went back to my Bible and read how Jesus Himself had been baptized in the Jordan. And I looked again at Paul's letter to the Romans where he talked about the rite in terms of death and resurrection. The "old man" dies, and a new creature arises, leaving all his sins behind.

Well, that was that. If Jesus was baptized, and if the Bible called for baptism, then of course I would obey.

That very moment I rang for Raisham.

"Please ask Manzur to get the car ready," I said. "I'm going to visit the Olds after lunch."

Shortly I was once again seated in Marie and Ken's small living room when I burst forth in my usual way. "Ken," I said, facing him squarely, "I'm sure that the Lord has told me to be baptized."

He looked at me for a long moment, his brow furrowing, perhaps trying to fathom the depth of my intention. Then Ken leaned forward and said, very, very seriously: "Bilquis, are you prepared for what may happen?"

"Yes, but . . ." I started to answer. Ken interrupted, his voice low.

"Bilquis, a Pakistani I met the other day asked if I were a sweeper in my own country." He looked at me levelly. "Do you realize that from now on you would not be *the* Begum Sheikh, the respected landowner with generations of prestige? From now on you will be associated with the sweeper Christians here?"

"Yes," I answered. "I do know that."

His words became still firmer and I steeled myself to look directly at him.

"And do you know," he continued, "that Mahmud's father can easily take him away from you? He could label you an unfit guardian."

My heart was stung. I had worried about this, but hearing Ken say it aloud made the prospect sound all the more possible.

"Yes, I know, Ken," I said weakly. "I realize many people will think I am committing a crime. But I want to be baptized, I must obey God."

Our conversation was interrupted by the unexpected arrival of the Mitchells. Ken immediately told them we had something important to discuss. "Bilquis," he said, "wants to be baptized."

Silence. Synnove coughed.

"But we don't have a tank for it," said David.

"How about the church in Peshawar?" asked Marie. "Don't they have a tank?"

My heart sank. Peshawar is the capital of the North-West Frontier Province. In every sense of the word it is frontier territory, a provincial town populated by conservative Muslims noted for their quickness to take action. Well, I thought, there goes any secrecy I might want to keep. The whole town would know within an hour.

It was left that Ken would make arrangements for us to go to Peshawar. We should hear from the pastor there in a day or two.

That evening my phone rang. It was my Grand Uncle Fateh. I loved this elderly gentleman dearly. He was always so interested in my religious instruction.

"Bilquis?" My uncle's authoritative voice sounded upset.

"Yes, Uncle?"

"Is it true that you are reading a Bible?"

"Yes." I wondered how he knew. What else had he heard?

Uncle Fateh cleared his throat. "Bilquis, don't *ever* talk about the Bible with any of these Christians. You know how argumentative they are. Their arguments always lead to confusion."

I started to interrupt him but he rode over my words. "Don't invite anyone . . . ," he emphasized ". . . *anyone* to your house without consulting me! If you do, you know that your family will not stand by you."

Uncle Fateh was quiet for a moment as he paused to catch his breath. I took advantage of the opening.

"Uncle, listen to me." There was a strained silence on the other end of the wire. I plunged ahead. "Uncle, as you'll remember, no one has ever entered my home without an invitation." My uncle would remember, all right; I was well known for ruthlessly refusing to see callers who had not arranged their visits beforehand.

"You know," I concluded, "that I will meet whomever I like. Goodbye, Uncle."

I hung up the phone. Was this an omen of things to

come as far as the rest of my family was concerned? If Uncle Fateh reacted so strongly just hearing that I read the Bible, what would happen when he and the rest of my family learned about my baptism? I didn't like to think.

Which only added fuel to my drive to be baptized right away. I wasn't sure I *could* resist pressure from scores of people I loved.

No word came from Ken.

The next morning as I was reading the Bible, I again ran across the story of the Ethiopian eunuch to whom Philip had brought the message of God. The first thing the eunuch did, as soon as he saw water, was to jump down out of the carriage to be baptized. It was as if the Lord was telling me all over again, "Get your baptism and get it now!" I felt sure He meant that if I waited much longer, something or someone might prevent it.

I leaped from my bed, realizing with fresh power that huge forces were marshalling to block me from what the Lord wanted me to do. I put down the Bible, summoned my maids who quickly dressed me and shortly I was speeding to the Mitchells'.

"David," I said, while we were still standing in the doorway, "is there any answer from Peshawar?"

"No, not as yet."

My voice rose. "Can't you baptize me here? Today? Now?"

David frowned. He ushered me in out of the cold morning air. "Now, Bilquis, we can't be in too much of a hurry about such a big step."

"I must obey my Lord. He keeps telling me to press on." I told him about my morning Bible reading, and about the new insistence from the Lord that He wanted me baptized before anything happened to me.

David held out his hands in helplessness. "I must take Synnove up to Abbottabad this afternoon and there isn't anything I can do now, Bilquis."

He put his hand on my arm. "Be patient, Bilquis. I'm sure we'll hear from Peshawar tomorrow."

I drove over to the Olds'.

"Please," I cried as Ken and Marie greeted me, "is there any way for me to be baptized immediately?"

"We asked our pastor," Ken said, taking me by the arm and leading me into the living room. "He says the whole matter has to go through the Session."

"Session?" I echoed. "What is that?"

He explained that his pastor wanted to baptize me but he had to get approval from his church's governing board. "This could take up to several days," he added, "and meanwhile anything could happen."

"Yes," I sighed, "word *would* get out." My mind raced desperately over all the possible circumstances.

Then Ken told me an amazing thing. In the middle of the night he had heard a man's voice directing him to *"Turn to page 654 in your Bible."* What a strange way, he thought, of giving a Bible reference. It was Job 13 and 14, and the verses shone out from the page. He read the verses that had so blessed him and which seemed meant for me. They started: *Wherefore do I take my flesh in my teeth, and put my life in mine hand? Though he slay me, yet will I trust in him.*

Was I ready for even *this*, I wondered? Was my trust *that* strong? I stood up and took Ken's arm. "Give me my water baptism now. And then, though He kill me, I am ready. I'll be better off in Heaven with my Lord."

I slumped down into a chair and looked up at Ken, apologizing. "I'm sorry, Ken. I'm getting upset. But one thing I know: the Lord said I should be baptized now. I shall put it to you bluntly. Are you going to help me or not?"

Ken sat back in his chair, ran his hand through his sandy brown hair. "Of course," he said, looking at Marie. "Why don't we go to the Mitchells' and see if there isn't something we can do?"

We drove back across the winding streets of Wah. For a while we sat quietly with the Mitchells in their living room in prayer. Then Ken sighed deeply, leaned forward and spoke to all of us. "I'm sure we all agree God has been guiding Bilquis in a most unusual way up until now. And if she insists her urgency to be baptized is from God, then let us not be a hindrance to her." He turned to David. "You're going to Abbottabad. Why don't Marie and I take Bilquis up there today, meet you and Synnove, and arrange for Bilquis' baptism there this afternoon? We'll forget about Peshawar."

Suddenly, it seemed the right thing to do and we all started making preparations. I hurried home, had Raisham pack an extra set of clothes which the Olds said I would need. "Something water won't hurt," Ken said.

Yet in the midst of all this I still felt uneasy. I even sensed the waning of my closeness to the Lord. Hadn't He in so many ways given me a specific urgent instruction? Hadn't He directed me to have my water baptism *now?*

A thought flicked through my mind. I dispelled the idea. It was unthinkable.

But when the thought persisted I asked my Lord in prayer: "Would it be all right, Father God?"

And thus on January 24, 1967, began a most unusual baptism.

Raisham stood before me, in answer to my call.

"Yes, Raisham," I said again. "Please fill the tub."

She turned to her duty, a puzzled expression on her face; never had I taken a bath at this hour of the day.

Raisham announced that my tub was ready; I dismissed her. What I proceeded to do may have some theological problems. But I wasn't thinking in theological terms. I was simply trying to be obedient to a strong urge which was backed up by Scripture. I was supposed to be baptized *now,* and with the impediments that I felt marshalling themselves, I had doubts about waiting even until the afternoon.

So, because I wanted more than anything else in the world to stay in the Lord's Presence, and the way to do that was through obedience, I walked into the bathroom and stepped into the deep tub. As I sat down, water rose almost to my shoulder. I placed my hand on my own head and said loudly: "Bilquis, I baptize you in the name of the Father and of the Son and of the Holy Ghost." I pressed my head down into the water so that my whole body was totally immersed.

I arose from the water rejoicing, calling out, and praising God. "Oh Father, thank You. I'm so fortunate." I *knew* that my sins had been washed away and that I was acceptable in the sight of the Lord.

I did not try to explain to Raisham what I had done and in her usual reserved manner she pointedly did not ask. Within a few minutes I was dressed, waiting for the Olds to take me to my baptism in Abbottabad. Again I didn't know what the theology of the situation was. I did know my motives. These Christian friends had taken such care of me, helping me. They had gone through a lot for me and I didn't want to confuse matters further. I would go ahead with the baptism, although some untrained instinct told me I had already done what the Lord wanted of me. I tried to read the Bible but my Spirit rejoiced so that I was unable to concentrate. I was back in the Glory again, just as I always was when I obeyed Him explicitly, with the Bible as my only check.

"Begum Sahib, Begum Sahib?"

I looked up. It was Raisham. The Olds were downstairs, waiting.

I told Mahmud I would be away for the rest of the day. I felt it better if he were not too involved in an event that might have unpleasant consequences. Then I went down to join Ken and Marie.

It was a two-hour drive to Abbottabad, along a road that was lined with firs and pines. I didn't mention my tub baptism. Instead I told about the many times I had travelled this same road on family outings, followed by several autos piled high with luggage. Silently I wondered if I should feel disloyal to this old heritage.

We arrived at the mission to find the Mitchells waiting with a Canadian medical doctor and his wife, Bob and Madeline Blanchard, who were our hosts. Along with them stood a Pakistani man. "This gentleman," said Synnove, "is Padri Bahadur, the minister who will baptize you."

I looked around at the others, including an Anglican doctor and another Pakistani minister.

"Perhaps this is prophetic, Bilquis," said Synnove. "Perhaps through you many Christians will be drawn closer, for this may be the first time in Pakistan that Baptists and Presbyterians and Anglicans have all gotten together in a common baptism."

There was an air of excitement about the room. Doors were closed, shades were drawn and I imagined what it was like back in the first century when Christians had their baptisms in the catacombs under Rome.

As we prepared for the ceremony, I looked around and asked, "But where is the tank?"

It developed there was none. Ken said that I would have to be sprinkled.

"But Jesus was immersed in the Jordan," I said.

We had crossed a river just before arriving at the mission station. "Why not take me back to the river?" I asked, but then I remembered that it was bitterly cold and others would have to get into that water too and I didn't press the point. Especially since I was certain that I had already received the sacrament.

And so I was baptized again, this time by sprinkling. While I was being sprinkled, I thought how the Lord must be chuckling. After the ceremony, I looked up to see tears streaming down the faces of others in the room. "Well," I laughed, "all this crying certainly doesn't encourage me!"

"Oh Bilquis," sniffed Synnove, coming up to throw her arms around me. She couldn't go on.

"Congratulations," said each of the others. Synnove sang a hymn, Ken read from the Bible, and then it was time to head for home again.

It was a quiet drive. There was no anxiety amongst us; it felt good just to be with Christians. We all said goodbye again amid tears, and I went into my house.

The comfortable mood was shattered as soon as I stepped through the door. The housekeeper rushed up to me, eyes wide, anxiety in her voice.

"Oh Begum Sahib, your family has been here asking about you! They say they know that you are mixing with Christians and. . . ."

I put up my hand. "Now stop!" I commanded, silencing the chatter. "Tell me who came."

As the housekeeper recited the names of those who had come to my house that day, a new apprehension filled me. These were the senior members of my family, uncles, elderly cousins, aunts, people who would come to my house in this manner only on a vitally important concern.

My heart sank. That night I ate with Mahmud, trying not to show my own fears, but just as soon as he went to bed I retired to my own room. I looked out the filigreed window; the snow had stopped falling and under the winter moon I could make out the outlines of the garden I loved. All around me I sensed the comfort of the old house I loved so much, my sanctuary, my retreat.

And now? Would I even be able to keep my home? It was a strange thought, for I had always had the security of family, money and prestige. Yet I felt without doubt that it was also a prophetic thought. The forces which I knew to be marshalling against me had already begun to express themselves through my family. Much of my "power," much of my "security" lay in the family. What would happen if suddenly they all began, at once, to oppose me?

Surely this was the very reason the Lord insisted that I have my baptism quickly, immediately. He knew me. He knew where I was most vulnerable.

I stood there looking out the window. Shadows from swaying trees played through the filigree.

"Oh Lord," I prayed, "please don't let them descend on me all at once. Please let them come one at a time."

No sooner had I breathed these words when there was a knock at the door. The downstairs maid came in to hand me a package. "This was just delivered for you," she said. Impatiently I tore off the wrapping to find a Bible. Inscribed on the fly leaf was: *To our dear sister on her birthday*— It was signed: "Ken and Marie Old."

I held it to my breast, thanking God for such good friends. Then I opened it and my eye was attracted to a page on which these words seemed to stand out: *I will scatter them abroad. . . .*

At the moment the meaning of these words was a mystery to me.

8.

Was There Protection?

I awakened the next morning full of apprehension. Today the family would come again, either en masse or one at a time. Either way I dreaded the awful confrontation. I dreaded the accusations, the angry warnings, the lures and threats which I knew were coming. Above all, I hated hurting them.

Not quite believing that God would answer my request, I had Raisham bring out my finest saris, chose the most attractive, issued word to the gate servant that I would be happy to see all visitors today, and then went to the drawing room. There I sat on one of the white silk chairs and read while Mahmud played with his toy cars, weaving them in and out of the paisley design of the large Persian rug on the floor.

The giant carved clock in the hall struck ten o'clock, eleven, and finally noon. Well, I thought, it looks as if they plan an afternoon visit.

Lunch was served and then while Mahmud napped I continued waiting. At last at three o'clock I heard the sound of a car stopping outside. I was steeling myself for battle when the car drove away! What was happening? I asked the maid and she said it was just someone making a delivery.

Evening darkened the tall windows of the drawing room

and shadows gathered high on the ceiling. Then there was a phone call for me. I glanced at the clock; it was seven. Were they phoning instead of coming in person?

I picked up the phone to hear a soft voice I recognized very well—Marie Old. She sounded quite worried. Word of my conversion was certainly out already, as yesterday's invasion of relatives showed. So why the concern?

"Are you all right?" Marie said. "I've been anxious about you."

I assured her that I was fine. As soon as I hung up the phone, I called for my wraps and asked that the car be sent around. At this time of the year, my family did not normally visit after eight o'clock so I felt it was safe to leave. Odd, how not one relative had called or visited.

I wanted reassurance from one of my Christian family. The Olds? Why had Marie called so mysteriously? I drove to the Olds' house and was surprised to find it completely dark.

And then, quite unexpectedly, quite abruptly, I was alarmed. As I stood at the gate leading into their yard I could feel fear settle over me, touching me with clammy cold horror. Dark thoughts came at me from dark corners of the yard. Surely I had been foolish to come out alone at night! What was that back in the shadows? My heart raced.

I turned. I was about to run for the car.

And then I stopped. No! This was no way to be acting. If I were a part of the Kingdom, I had a right to the King's protection. Standing there in the awesome darkness, still very much afraid, I deliberately willed myself back into the King's hands. "Jesus. Jesus. Jesus." I said over and over again. Incredibly the fear lifted. As soon as it had come, it was gone. I was free!

Almost smiling now, I turned toward the Olds' house. After a few paces, I saw a crack of light coming between two drawn curtains in the living room. I knocked.

The door slowly opened. It was Marie. When she saw

me she gave a sigh of relief and quickly drew me into the house and hugged me.

"Ken! Ken!" she called.

He was there in a moment. "Oh thank God!" he exclaimed. "We were quite worried about you." Ken told me that the Pakistani Padri at my baptism had become quite concerned for my safety and had told them that they had made a mistake in leaving me alone.

"So, that's why you were so concerned on the phone, Marie!" I suppressed a nervous laugh. "Well, I expect the whole country will soon know about my conversion, but thank you anyhow. So far, nothing has happened. Even my family didn't show up and you can't know how grateful I am for that answer to prayer."

"Let's thank the Lord," Ken said, and the three of us knelt together in their living room as Ken thanked God for my protection and asked Him to continue to watch over me.

So, I returned home, the richer for having called on God's help in the face of fear by taking advantage of the Name of Jesus. My servants said there had not been a phone call all that evening. Well, I thought as I prepared for bed, watch out for tomorrow.

Again, I waited in the drawing room all day, praying, thinking, studying the white mosaic floor tiles and the paisley print of the Persian rugs. There was not a word from anyone.

What was going on? Was this some kind of a cat and mouse game?

And then I thought to check with the servants. In Pakistan if you want to know anything, ask a household servant. Through an uncanny grapevine, they know everything about everybody.

Finally, I pinned down my handmaid Nur-jan: "Tell me, what happened to my family?"

"Oh Begum Sahib," she answered, suppressing a nervous giggle, "the strangest thing happened. It was as if everybody was busy at once. Your brother had to go to the annual Winter Cricket Tournament." I smiled; to my brother, cricket was more important than a sister who was on her way to hell. "Your Uncle Fateh had to go out of the province on a court case; your Aunt Amina needed to go to Lahore; two of your cousins were called out of town on business, and . . ."

I stopped her; she need not go on any further. The Lord had said He would scatter them and scatter them He did. I could almost hear my Lord chuckle. It wasn't, I felt sure, that the concerned members of my family would leave me alone, but now they would come one by one.

And so it was. The first emissary was my Aunt Amina, a regal woman in her seventies whose eastern beauty somehow always looked out of place in my drawing room with its modern western furniture. For years we had a close relationship of love and trust. Now as she walked in, her magnolia complexion was paler than usual and her gray eyes were rimmed with sadness.

We chatted a bit. Finally I could tell she was coming to the real reason for her visit. Clearing her throat, she sat back and, trying to sound casual, asked: "Er . . . Bilquis . . . uh . . . I have heard . . . that you have become a Christian. Is it true?"

I only smiled at her.

She shifted uneasily in her chair and continued. "I thought people were spreading false rumors about you." She hesitated, her soft eyes imploring me to say that it wasn't true.

"It is no lie, Aunt Amina," I said. "I have made a complete commitment to Christ. I have been baptized. I am now a Christian."

She slapped her hands over her cheeks. "Oh, what a great mistake!" she cried. She sat very still for a moment, unable to add anything. Then, slowly gathering her shawl around her, she stood and with frozen dignity walked out of my house.

I was crushed, but I asked the Lord to protect her from

the devastating hurt she was feeling. I knew I had to discover His own prayer for my family. Otherwise, I would leave a swath of damaged loved ones behind me. "Lord," I said, "the ideal thing of course would be to have every one of these people come to know You. But I know that if they aren't converted, I know You still love them, and right now I ask that You touch each of these dear ones of mine with Your special blessing, starting, if You will, with my Aunt Amina. Thank You, Lord!"

Next day I had to say the same prayer. This time it was for Aslam, a dear elderly male cousin who came to see me. A lawyer, he lived about 45 miles from Wah. As the son of my father's brother, he had inherited many of my father's characteristics, the same warm smile, the gentle sense of humor. I was fond of Aslam. From his attitude, I was sure that he had not heard the full particulars of my problem. We exchanged a few pleasantries, and then Aslam said:

"When is the family meeting? I'll pick you up and we'll go together."

I chuckled. "I don't know when the family meeting will be, Aslam, but I do know that I'll not be invited because the meeting is about me."

He looked so confused I knew that I had to explain everything. "But please go to the meeting, Aslam," I said, when I had finished. "Maybe you can put in a good word for me."

I watched him sadly make his way out of the house; it was obvious, I thought, that a climax was approaching. I had better get to Rawalpindi and Lahore as soon as possible. I didn't want Tooni and my son Khalid to hear garbled stories about me. There was nothing I could do in person about my daughter Khalida, for she lived in Africa. But I could face Khalid and Tooni. The very next day I set off for Lahore. Khalid had done quite well in business, and his home reflected it. A lovely town bungalow, it was surrounded by wide verandas and an immaculately groomed lawn.

We drove through his gate, parked by the entrance and

walked up onto the broad veranda. Khalid well alerted by family and by a long phone call from me, hurried out to greet me. "Mother! How glad I am to see you," he said, though I sensed he welcomed me with a little embarrassment. We talked all that afternoon about what I had done, but in the end I knew Khalid did not understand at all.

Next I had to see Tooni. I drove to Rawalpindi and went straight to the hospital. I asked that Tooni be paged, and as I waited I wondered how I should go about telling her. Doubtless she had been hearing stories already. She certainly was aware firsthand that I had been reading the Bible. She may even have overheard fragments of my conversation with the Catholic nun, Dr. Santiago, in this same hospital when Mahmud had been admitted. One thing she surely did *not* know: how life-changing that visit with Dr. Santiago had been, for it was this little nun who encouraged me to pray to God as my Father.

"Mother!" I looked up to see Tooni hurrying toward me, her chestnut hair in stark contrast to her white starched uniform, her face beaming, her arms outstretched.

I rose, my heart pounding. How was I going to break the news to her! I tried to think of gentle ways, but the fear of pressure from Tooni was too much. Without daring to be circumspect, I blurted it out. "Tooni," I said, "be prepared for a shock, dear. Two days ago I was . . . I was *baptized.*"

Tooni froze, her hand half extended, her sensitive eyes filling with tears. She slumped on the couch next to me. "I thought it would be coming to this," she said in a voice I could hardly hear.

I tried to comfort her, with no success. "There's no point in pretending to work," Tooni said. So she got permission to leave early and together we drove over to her apartment. Tooni's phone was ringing as she unlocked the door; she rushed in, picked the receiver up, and turned to me. "It's Nina." This was a niece who also lived in Rawalpindi. "She wants to know if it's true." She turned back to the phone as

Nina had evidently started talking again; even from where I stood I could hear Nina's voice rising. Then Tooni said softly: "Yes, it's true Nina. She's done it." Nina must have slammed down the phone, because Tooni took the receiver from her ear, looked at it, shrugged, and slowly replaced it on its cradle. It would be best to give her time to collect her thoughts. So I collected my things.

"Come see me, darling," I said, "when you feel you can. We'll talk." Tooni made no objections at all, so within minutes I was on the Grand Trunk Road headed home. The minute I arrived home my servants clustered around me. Nur-jan was wringing her plump hands and even Raisham's face was paler than usual. The phone had been ringing all day, relatives had been at the gate since early morning asking for me. Even as the servants chattered, the phone rang again. It was my sister's husband, Jamil, who worked with a British oil firm. I had always thought of Jamil as a man of the world, but now his voice didn't sound very self-assured.

"Bilquis, I have heard the strangest thing and cannot believe it," he said bluntly. "A business friend told me that he heard you had become a Christian. Of course, I laughed at him and assured him that could never happen."

Word really was spreading rapidly. I said nothing.

"Bilquis!" Jamil's voice was insistent. "Did you *hear* me?"

"Yes."

"That story isn't true is it?"

"Yes."

There was another silence. Then: "Well, that's nice," Jamil snapped. "You've just lost more than you can know. And for what? For just another religious viewpoint. That's what." He hung up.

In ten minutes Tooni was on the phone sobbing. "Mama, Uncle Nawaz just called to say that now Mahmud's father will be able to get him back. Nawaz says no court will allow you to keep him!"

I tried to comfort her but she hung up sobbing.

Late that evening while Mahmud and I were dining in my bedroom, Tooni and two of my nieces came to the house. I was startled by their ashen faces.

"Please sit down and join me," I said. "I'll have the servants bring your meal up."

Tooni and my nieces just picked at their food. I was happy to see the two young girls, but it was clear they weren't happy to see me. The conversation was trite and all three women kept glancing at Mahmud and making oblique suggestions that he go away to play. It was only after he finally did leave that one of the nieces leaned forward anxiously.

"Auntie, do you realize what this means for *other* people?" She broke into tears. "Have you thought of anybody else?" Her question was echoed in the brown eyes of my other niece who sat silently across from me.

I reached across the table and took the girl's slim hand. "My dear," I said sorrowfully. "There is nothing I can do but to be obedient."

Tooni now looked at me through tearful eyes and, as if she had not heard a word I said, begged me. "Mother, pack up and leave. Leave while there's something . . . or some-one . . . to leave with."

Her voice rose. "Do you know what people are saying? You'll be attacked. Your own brother may be compelled to take action against you!" And then she broke down sobbing. "My friends say you'll be murdered, Mommy!"

"I'm sorry, Tooni, but I'm not going to run away," I answered gently. "If I leave now I'll be running for the rest of my life." Determination rose within me as I spoke. "If He wishes, God can easily take care of me in my own house. And no one, *no one*," I said, "is going to push me out." I sat up in my chair, suddenly feeling very dramatic. "Let them come and attack!"

And then, as I sat there feeling so fiercely sure of myself, something happened. The warm personal Presence of God was gone. I sat, almost in panic, oblivious to the voices rising around me. But just as suddenly I realized what had happened. The old me, full of pride and stubbornness, had taken over. *I* was deciding what would happen, that no one would push me out of my home.

I sank back in my chair, barely aware that Tooni was speaking to me.

". . . all right, then, Mommy," Tooni cried. "So you've become a Christian. Must you become a Christian martyr also?" She knelt by my chair and laid her head on my shoulder. "Don't you realize that we love you?"

"Of course, dear, of course," I murmured, stroking her hair. Silently I asked His forgiveness for being so headstrong. Wherever He wanted me to go was fine, even if it meant leaving my house. As I said this in my heart I once again felt the Presence of the Father. The whole exchange had taken but a few minutes, but even as the three women sitting in front of me continued talking, I was aware that life was going on at another level too. The Lord was right then, at that moment, working with me, teaching me. He was in the very process of showing me how to stay in His Presence.

". . . so we will, then? All right?" It was Tooni's voice and I had no idea what she was asking me to agree to. Fortunately she went on. "If Mahmud's father comes after him, you can let me take him. I haven't become a Christian," she added pointedly.

Eventually the three girls quieted down. I asked them if they wouldn't like to spend the night and they agreed. As I bid Tooni and my nieces goodnight, I thought how our roles had changed. Once I was so protective and worried over them; now we were equally worried for each other. That night I prayed: "Lord, it's so difficult to talk to a person who doesn't have faith in You. Please help my family. I'm so worried for the welfare of my loved ones."

As I drifted off to sleep, I again seemed to have left my body as if floating. I found myself standing on a grassy slope surrounded by pine trees. A spring bubbled near me.

All about me were angels, so many that they seemed to form a hazy mist. I kept hearing one name, "Saint Michael!". The angels gave me courage. And then I was back in bed. I got up and, still sensing this spiritual strength, went to Mahmud's room. I pointed to him in his bed and then went to my daughter's and nieces' rooms and did the same. I went back to my bedroom and got down on my knees. "Lord," I prayed, "You have shown me so many answers, now show me, I pray, what You are going to do with Mahmud. I would like to give Tooni some assurance."

I felt urged to open my Bible and this passage leaped up from the page: Genesis 22:12—"Lay not thine hand upon the lad, neither do thou anything unto him. . . ."

"Oh, thank You Father," I sighed.

At breakfast I was able to assure Tooni. "Darling, nothing is going to happen to your son; you never need worry." I showed her the Scripture given to me. Whether my faith was contagious or Tooni was touched by the Holy Spirit, I don't know. But her face did relax and she smiled for the first time in two days.

My daughter and nieces left my house on a somewhat less somber note that day. But the flow of other relatives and friends continued.

A few days later Raisham announced that there were *seven* people, all very dear concerned friends downstairs wanting to see me. I didn't want to face them without Mahmud. The boy should know everything that was going on. So I found him and together we went downstairs to the drawing room. There they sat in straight-backed formality far forward on their chairs. After the tea and cakes and small talk, one of those present cleared his throat. I steeled myself for what I knew was coming.

"Bilquis," said a friend I'd known since childhood, "we love you and we have been thinking over this thing you have done and we have a suggestion which we think will be of help to you."

"Yes?"

He leaned forward and smiled.

"Don't declare your Christianity publicly."

"You mean keep my faith a secret?"

"Well . . ."

"I can't," I said. "I can't play games with God. If I must die, I die."

All seven of them seemed to edge closer to me. An old friend of my father glared at me. I was about to glare back but caught myself. They thought they had my welfare at heart.

"I'm sorry," I said, "I just can't do what you ask." I explained that my faith had quickly, in little more than a month, become the most important thing in my life. "I cannot keep quiet about it," I said. I quoted them the Scripture where the Lord says: "Every man who publicly acknowledges me I shall acknowledge in the presence of my Father in Heaven, but the man who disowns me before men I shall disown before my Father in Heaven" (Matthew 10:32, 33).

"But," said another elderly gentleman, "you are in a very peculiar situation. I'm sure your God wouldn't mind if you kept quiet. He knows you believe in Him. That's enough." He quoted the Koran law on apostasy. "We're afraid," he said, "that someone will kill you."

I smiled but no one else was smiling. It was a pointless discussion, as they saw. When they rose to go I was given my ultimatum.

"Remember, Bilquis, if you get into trouble, none of your friends or family can stand by you. The ones who care the most will have to turn their backs on you."

I nodded. I well understood their words. I wished now that I had sent Mahmud out to play in the garden so that he would have heard none of this. When I looked at him, though, sitting on his little chair beside me, he just smiled. "It's all right," he seemed to be saying.

There were near tears as the group prepared to leave. A close friend of my mother kissed me. "Goodbye," she said.

She repeated the word with a strange emphasis. Then she broke into tears, pulled herself away and hurried out the door.

The house seemed like a tomb after they left. Even Mahmud's usual noisy play was subdued.

Three weeks passed when the only sound in my house was the hushed voices of servants. If it weren't for the Mitchells and the Olds and for our regular Sunday evening meetings, I wonder if the freeze-out might not have worked.

Each day the family battle line was seen more clearly. I saw it in the anger on the face of a cousin I met in the bazaar. I felt it in the scornful glance of a nephew I passed on the street in Rawalpindi. It was there in the cold voice of an aunt who called to say that she wouldn't keep a luncheon appointment. The boycott had begun. My phone remained silent, and no one pulled the bell cord at my gate. Not one member of the family came to call, even to scold. I could not help but recall a verse from the Koran (Sura 74-20): *If you renounced the faith, you would surely do evil in the land and violate the ties of blood. Such are those on whom Allah has laid His curse leaving them bereft of sight and hearing.*

In a very real way this was happening. I had violated the ties of blood and I undoubtedly would not see or hear from my family anymore.

The normal chatter and laughter of the servants had quieted as they slipped in and out of my rooms. I could hardly get them to talk to me beyond the usual, "Yes, Begum Sahib."

And then one morning the boycott took a strange turn. There was a soft click of my door and I turned to see Nur-jan quietly enter to minister my toilette. It was so unlike her usual exuberance. Raisham stepped in even more solemn than usual. As they proceeded to their tasks, they did not speak and I was bothered by the haunted look on both of their faces.

I waited for some word but Nur-jan continued her tasks

silently, without the usual gossip or chatter. Raisham's face was graven. Finally, with a little of the old fire in my voice, I said:

"All right, I can tell something is wrong. Tell me about it."

The brushing halted as I heard the news. Except for Raisham, standing before me now, all of my Christian servants, including Manzur, had fled my house in the middle of the night.

9.

The Boycott

What did it mean, this defection? Four servants quitting! In a town like Wah where any job was hard to come by, their decisions were hard to understand.

It was fear of course. Manzur was afraid because I asked him to get me a Bible and had him drive me to the home of missionaries. The other three Christian servants must have picked up his concern. They must have heard the rumblings of a volcano which would soon erupt and didn't want to be caught in the overflow.

But what about Raisham, this Christian servant who now began to brush my hair again? I could feel her graceful hands tremble as she started her work.

"And you?" I asked.

She bit her lip as she continued her brushing. "I probably shouldn't stay," she said softly. "It's going to be . . ."

"Very lonely," I concluded her statement.

"Yes," she said, swallowing, "and . . ."

"And you're afraid. Well, if you left, Raisham, I wouldn't blame you. You have to make up your own mind, just as I did. If you do stay though, remember that Jesus *told* us we would be persecuted for His sake."

Raisham nodded, her dark eyes moist. She took a hairpin out of her mouth and proceeded to do up my hair. "I know," she said sadly.

94

Raisham was quiet the rest of the day. Her concern affected Nur-jan who was approaching quiet hysteria. The next morning when I awakened I could hardly bring myself to ring the little bell. Who would be with me now? My bedroom door opened slowly and Nur-jan came in. Then, in the near darkness of winter's early hours another form followed. It was Raisham!

Later, I told her how much I appreciated her staying. She blushed. "Begum Sahib Gi," she answered softly, adding the affectionate third salutation which means, May you have long life, "as you serve the Lord, so I will serve you."

With the rest of my Christian servants gone, my house became even quieter, partly because I did not replace them all. My needs were simpler now that no family came by. I decided not to rehire Christians for a while. I found a new chauffeur, a Muslim named Fazad and a new Muslim cook's assistant, but I hired no one else. I was especially glad for Mahmud who continued to play happily in the house or garden. I encouraged him to invite friends over from the village, which suggestion Mahmud accepted quickly. Most of the children were slightly older, five or six, while Mahmud was still only five. But Mahmud nevertheless was their natural leader; I didn't think it was simply that he was their host, rather that seven hundred years of leadership was in the child's genes and could no more be denied than could his limpid brown eyes.

How much of this heritage was I putting in jeopardy? How much of the boy's rightful family ties was I threatening? Just yesterday he had asked again when his cousin Karim was going to take him fishing. Karim had promised to teach Mahmud the mysteries of catching the trout that slipped among the mossy rocks of our garden stream which joined the Tahmra River.

"Mum!" Mahmud had asked. "When is Karim going to come?"

I looked down at the boy whose eyes were shining, and I just didn't have the heart to tell him that his fishing party would never take place. Mahmud could not have been very drawn to Christianity so far. I read him Bible stories which he loved so much that I moved his bedtime from 8:00 to 7:30 so we could have plenty of time for them. But what were a few stories compared with a fishing trip. And friends. For bit by bit Mahmud's friends began to stop coming over. Mahmud couldn't understand this, and when I tried to explain it to him he looked at me in puzzlement.

"Mum," he said, "who do you love better, me or Jesus?"

What should I say! Especially right now when he was lonely. "God has to come first, Mahmud." I said, paraphrasing the Lord's warning that unless we put family after Him, we are not truly His own. "We have to put God first," I said, "even before the people we love most in the world."

Mahmud *seemed* to accept this. He *seemed* to be listening when I read him the Bible. Once, after I had read to him, "Come unto me all ye who are heavy laden and I will give you rest," I heard his nap-time pleas: "Jesus, I love You and I will come unto You, but . . . please don't give me rest. I don't like resting." He would even fold his hands and pray, but I knew that it was hard on him being alone and seeing me alone. Not one relative, friend or acquaintance turned off of the Grand Trunk Road any more toward my house; never did the phone ring.

Then at 3:00 one morning my white bedside phone did clamor. I reached toward the instrument, my heart pounding. No one would call at this hour unless there had been a death in the family. I picked up the phone and at first heard only heavy breathing. Then three words were thrown at me like stones:

"Infidel. Infidel. Infidel."

The phone went dead. I lay back on my bed. Who was it? One of the fanatics my uncles constantly warned me about? What might they do?

"Oh Lord, You know that I don't mind dying. But I'm an awful coward. I cannot stand pain. You know how I faint when the doctor gives me a needle. Oh, I pray that I will be able to bear pain if it comes." Tears filled my eyes. "I guess I'm not made of the stuff of martyrs, Lord. I'm sorry. Just let me walk with You through whatever comes next."

What did come next was a threatening, anonymous letter. "Let's be clear. There is only one word to describe you. Traitor." Then there was another letter and shortly still another. They all contained warnings. I was a turncoat and I would be treated as such.

Late one afternoon in the early summer of 1967, about six months after my conversion, I stood in my garden with the crumpled remains of one such letter in my fist. It was particularly vitriolic, calling me worse than an infidel, a seducer of the faithful. True believers, the letter said, had to burn me out like gangrene was burned out of a healthy limb.

Burn me out? Was this more than just a figure? I walked further into the garden, around which glowed beds of tulips, hyacinth and alyssum. Spring had blossomed into summer. Quinces flourished in the garden, and the last of the white petals were falling from the pear trees. I turned and looked back at my house. "They wouldn't touch my house!" I exclaimed inwardly. They wouldn't burn out a Begum! But, as if to confirm that I could no longer count on the protection of position and wealth, a caller came to pay me a visit. He was announced by a servant.

"General Amar is waiting to see you, Begum," she said.

My heart jumped. I looked through the garden gate and sure enough, there stood a familiar olive drab command car. General Amar was a dear old friend from my Army days. During World War II, I had been associated with him and now he was a top general in the Pakistani Army. We had kept in touch with each other through the years, particularly when my husband was Minister of the Interior and worked closely with him. Was he, too, coming to condemn me?

Soon I could hear his footsteps crunching on the pathway of the garden as he strode to meet me, all spit and polish in a natty khaki uniform, jodhpurs and leather boots. He took my hand, leaned over and kissed it. My apprehension lessened; evidently he was not on a mission of battle.

He looked at me, his dark eyes glinting humorously. As always the General came right to the point. "Is it true what people are saying?"

"Yes," I said.

"What made you do this?" he exclaimed. "You've put yourself in a very dangerous situation! I've heard rumors that some people want to kill you!"

I looked at him silently.

"All right," he added as he sat down on a garden bench, his leather belt creaking. "You know I'm like a brother to you?"

"I hope so."

"And, as a brother, I feel fondly protective toward you?"

"I hope so."

"Then, remember that my home is always open to you."

I smiled. This was the first kind thing anyone had said to me.

"*But,*" the general went on to say, "there is something you should know. That offer is a personal one." He reached over to a blossom, pulled it to him and sniffed it, then turned back to me, adding, "Officially, there wouldn't be much I could do, Bilquis."

"I know." I took the General's hand, we got up together, strolled onto the terrace and inside the house. As we walked I told him things had not been easy.

"And they won't get easier, my dear," my friend said in his matter of fact way. Later, after I had ordered tea in the drawing room, he asked with a quizzical smile: "Tell me, Bilquis, why did you do it?"

I explained what had happened and found that General Amar was listening carefully. How extraordinary! Here I was, without realizing it, doing what the missionaries called *witnessing.* I was speaking about Christ to a Muslim, and a high official at that. And he was listening! I doubt that I really reached General Amar that afternoon but he was in a reflective mood half an hour later when he bid me goodbye in the summer twilight, again pressing his lips to my hand.

"Remember, Bilquis," he said huskily, "anytime you need my help . . . anything I can do as a friend . . ."

"Thank you, Amar," I said.

He turned, his boot heels clicked down the hallway tiles and out into the early evening darkness to his waiting command car. And our solitary, strangely sad, visit was over. "I wonder if I'll ever see him again," I thought.

For the first time during this boycott, during the anonymous letters and phone calls, during the warnings of old friends, I was learning what it was to live from hour to hour. It was the opposite of worrying. It was waiting to see *what He was going to allow.* For I was convinced that nothing occurred without His permission. I knew, for instance, that pressure against me must become more intense. If that did happen, then He would have allowed it and I must learn to search for His Presence in the midst of seeming disaster. I would just live hour to hour, staying near Him. Yes, that was my key. Learn to keep His company, so that whatever happened, whenever it happened, I would still be in His glory.

With the increasing family pressure, I thought I knew how King David felt when, fleeing from his son, Absalom, he picked up his lyre and sang: *"But thou, O Lord, art a shield for me; my glory . . ."* (Psalms 3:3). The glory which, I understand, he considered the unspeakable blessedness, joy, and felicity of the saints in heaven.

For the moment the pressure from my family was, still, the boycott. Not one member of the family came to call, even to scold. With rare exceptions none of my old friends called either. The sneers in the marketplace continued. So did the calculated exclusion from great moments in the family: births, deaths, weddings. Whenever I allowed myself to dwell on the loneliness this caused, I'd feel the glory begin to fade, and immediately I'd turn my thoughts by a sheer act of will to the times Jesus too had felt lonely.

It helped. But I found, a little to my surprise, that I desperately needed simple companionship. I who had been so aloof was now in need of closeness. Not even the Olds and the Mitchells came to the house anymore. For their own protection I advised them not to visit me.

One gray afternoon I retreated to my bedroom to read the Bible. It was unusually cold for early summer. A sharp wind rattled my windows. As I started to read, I felt a warmth on my hand and looked down to see a patch of sunlight resting on my arm. I glanced out of the window just in time to see the sun disappear again behind the clouds. For just one minute, it seemed He had reached down and touched my hand for comfort.

I looked up, "Oh my Lord," I said. "I am so lonely; even my cheeks feel dried up from lack of talking. Please send someone to talk to today."

Feeling somewhat foolish for asking for such a childlike thing, I returned to my Bible. After all, I had His company and that should be enough. But in a little while I was startled to hear an odd sound in the house, odd since it had been absent so long. There were voices downstairs.

I threw on my robe and flew out into the hall to meet Nur-jan running toward my room out of breath. "Oh, Begum Sahib," she squealed, "the Olds are here."

"Praise God," I exclaimed and hurried to meet them. Of course I saw Ken and Marie at our Sunday services in their house, but this was different, a midweek call. Marie rushed to me, taking my hand. "We just had to see you, Bilquis," she said, her blue eyes sparkling. "For no reason at all except we love being with you."

What a visit that was. I realized as we talked that I had been making a mistake not asking people over to visit me. Pride had kept me from admitting the need. Suddenly I had an inspiration. Why not invite people to my house on Sunday for the meetings? But wouldn't this be heaping gunpowder on the flames? I tried to quench the thought but it would not go away. Just as my friends were about to leave I said, quickly:

"Would you like to come here this Sunday night?"

The Olds looked at me a bit shocked.

"I mean it," I said, extending my hands sideways. "This old house needs some life."

And so it was decided.

That evening as I prepared to retire, I thought how wonderfully the Lord provides for us. When my family and friends were taken from me, He replaced them with His own family and friends. I slept peacefully and awakened to the feel of a warm sun streaming through my window. I got up and opened the window, reveling in the soft breeze that drifted in. In its earthy garden aroma I could smell the warm breath of the full summer now upon us.

I couldn't wait for Sunday evening to come. By Saturday afternoon that old house was filled with flowers; every floor, every window was scrubbed until it shown. I hinted to Raisham that she might like to join us but she became a bit flustered; she was not ready for such a bold step yet and I didn't press.

Sunday crept by while I kept Mahmud out of the drawing room, straightened the Persian carpet, constantly rearranged the flowers, and found a speck of dust here and there to wipe away. But at last I heard the gate open and cars crunch up the drive.

The evening was everything I had hoped for, with song and prayer and telling each other what the Lord was doing. Just twelve of us, plus Mahmud, sitting around comfortably in the drawing room, but I'd have sworn there were a thousand other guests too, unseen, welcome.

The evening had another peculiar purpose too, one I had not foreseen. It turned out that my Christian friends were still quite worried for me.

"Are you being extra careful?" It was Marie talking.

"Well," I laughed, "there is not much I can do. If someone wants to harm me, I'm sure he'll find a way."

Ken looked around the drawing room and out the large glass doors into the garden. "You really *don't* have much protection here," he said. "I hadn't quite realized how vulnerable you are."

"How about your bedroom?" asked Synnove. Everyone

felt it wise to look over my room, so we all trooped up. Ken was particularly concerned by the windows, looking out on the garden; they were protected only by a glass pane and filigree screen.

He shook his head. "It really isn't safe, you know. You should do something about it, Bilquis; have some kind of heavy metal grill installed. Anyone could get through this."

I said I would see to it the next day.

Was it my imagination or did His glory fade just a little as I made the promise?

Eventually we said goodbye and I retired happier than I had been in a long time. The next day, however, as I was about to send for the ironworker in the village, I was once again aware of the quickly receding glory of the Lord. Why? Was it because I was about to take an action that was based on fear? It certainly did seem that every time I started to call the ironworker my action was stopped.

And then I realized why. When word got around the village that I was having my window barred, everyone would realize that I was fearful. I could just hear the gossip. "Ha! What kind of religion is Christianity, anyway. When you become a Christian you become fearful?" No. I decided, I would not have the window barred.

That night I went to bed confident that I had made the right decision. I fell asleep at once but suddenly I was awakened by a sound. I sat up, startled, but without fear. Before me appeared a breathtaking sight.

Through the walls of my room, in a supernatural way, I could see my whole garden. It was flooded with a heavenly white light. I could see every rose petal, every tree leaf, every blade of grass, every thorn. And over the garden hung a calm serenity. In my heart I heard my Father saying, "You did the right thing, Bilquis. I am with you."

Slowly the light faded and the room was dark again. I switched on my bedside lamp, lifted my arms and praised God. "Oh Father, how can I thank You enough? You have so much concern for each of us."

The next morning I called all of my servants together and told them that they could sleep in their own homes from now on if they chose to do so. Only Mahmud and I would sleep in the big house. The servants exchanged glances, some in surprise, some in joy, one or two in alarm. But I knew one thing at least had been accomplished. The decision put an end to any thought of protecting myself. And with the decision the glory came back and stayed for a longer time than usual. Perhaps this was necessary for the next turn of events.

One morning when Raisham was brushing my hair she remarked casually: "I hear that your Aunt's son, Karim, has died."

I shot out of my chair and looked at her incredulously. "No," I gasped. Not Karim, who was supposed to take Mahmud fishing! He was one of my favorites! What had happened? Why did I have to find out about even Karim's death through the servants! With steely willpower I got control of myself and forced my body back down into the chair so that Raisham could go on with her work. But my mind raced on. This could be just a rumor, I thought. Raisham could have mistaken the name. My heart rose a little. Later, I asked an elderly member of the staff to find out for me what had really happened. She went into the village and in an hour returned, downcast.

"I am sorry, Begum Sahib," she said. "But it is true. He died last night from a heart attack and the funeral is to-day."

Then, this servant who had a facility for learning everything, gave me news that hurt even more. My aunt, the servant told me, knowing how much I loved her son, had specifically asked my family to "be sure and tell Bilquis that my boy has died." No one followed her wishes.

Later I sat at my window pondering it all. I had been excluded from family events for six months, but never had the boycott hurt as it did now.

As I sat rocking softly I began to pray for His help and, as always, the help came. This time it was as if a warm cloak were placed gently on my shoulders. And with that sensation came an unusual plan of action. The very idea shocked me. It was so bold I knew it must be of the Lord.

10.

Learning to Live in the Glory

As I sat at the window overlooking my garden, where Karim and I had played as children, a strong monsoon wind blowing up from India bent the tops of the trees. In it I seemed to be catching an extraordinary message which I could not believe I was correctly hearing.

"You can't really be telling me that Lord," I said smiling. "I'm just hearing voices! You don't want me to go to *Karim's funeral*. It would be unseemly. It would be in poor taste. I would end up offending people who are in mourning."

Even as I objected, I recognized once again the sense of His Presence beginning to fade. Immediately, with this sign, I began to wonder if perhaps I really were being told to do this extraordinary thing, to go straight into the face of the hostilities of the boycott.

Finally, breathing a deep sigh, I got up from my place at the window, shrugged and said aloud, "I'm beginning to learn, Lord. My sense of the right thing to do is nothing compared with Yours! I'll go, since You are telling me to go."

And, of course, the sense of His Presence returned.

What an extraordinary series of experiences I was having with this coming and going of His glory. Still, I had the feeling that I was just on the verge of understanding what this was all about. How would I be able to learn to stay in His Presence for an ever increasing percentage of time? I did not realize that over the next two months I was to have a series of experiences which would take me a step further in this learning process.

I stood in the cobblestone lane in front of Karim's house, hesitating. In spite of my promise to obey, I felt as if I were a lonesome dove being thrown to a thousand cobras. Taking a deep breath I headed toward the stone house which stood among others like it. I walked into the courtyard and stepped onto the veranda, subject to the stares of the village people who were sitting around quietly. I went inside the old-fashioned house with its carved ceilings and white plastered walls where Karim and I had so often laughed, played and romped together.

There was no laughter now. On top of the gloom of the family in mourning was added the chill of a score of contemptuous glances directed my way. I looked toward a cousin with whom I had been very close. Our eyes met for a minute; my cousin quickly turned her head and began talking with a neighbor.

Now squaring my shoulders I stepped into the living room of Karim's house, then sat down on one of the thick cotton mattresses which had been placed on the floor surrounded by bolsters and cushions to lean on. I smoothed the sari around my legs. Suddenly people seemed to wake up, realizing who I was. The quiet soothing conversation that had filled the room suddenly halted. Even the women saying their beads, each bead signifying a prayer to Allah, ceased and looked up. The room, which had been hot with the early summer heat and with the scores of bodies packed shoulder to shoulder, suddenly seemed chilled.

I said nothing, made no attempt to be sociable, simply lowered my own eyes and said my own prayers. "Lord

Jesus," I whispered to my heart, "do be with me as I represent You to this group of dear friends and relatives who are so saddened by Karim's death."

After fifteen minutes the quiet flow of conversation began again. It was time to pay my respects to Karim's wife. Holding my head high, I arose from the mattress and stepped into the adjoining room where Karim's body lay in its tall, deep coffin, structured according to the Muslim belief that a dead person must be able to sit up when the angels came to question him before he enters heaven. I gave my condolences to Karim's wife, then looked at the quiet face of my dear cousin shrouded in the new white cotton burial cloth and whispered to myself a prayer to Jesus for this man's spirit. Oh, how I wished I had been able to talk to him before he died.

A low humming filled the room as close family members prayed for Karim. The ladies stood and read verses from the Koran. It was all part of the life and death rhythm which I knew so well. I was turning my back on it all. Before sunset today, there would be a procession to the cemetery with all of the family following the bier. At the grave side the pallbearers would place the coffin on the ground and the priest would call out, *God is most great. Lord, this is Thy servant, the son of Thy servant. He used to testify that there is no God but Thee, and that Muhammad is Thy servant and Thy messenger. . . .*

As I stood listening to the soft moaning in the room, I saw Karim's mother kneeling at the bier. She looked so forlorn, I suddenly felt an overwhelming urge to go to her side. Did I dare? Would it be an affront? Should I say anything to her about Jesus? Probably not. Just my being there as a Christian was bringing Jesus to her side in a caring way.

So I stepped over to Karim's mother and put my arms around her, telling her in a soft crooning voice how sorry I was. "Karim and I were so close. May God bless you and comfort you." Karim's mother turned her face to me. Her dark tear-filled eyes thanked me and I knew that Jesus was even then comforting her sorrow-filled heart.

But Karim's mother was the only one in the room who seemed to accept what I was doing. As I left her and returned to sit down among the mourners, one male cousin —a close one too—made quite a show of rising to his feet and shuffling out of the room. Another cousin followed. And then another.

I sat there struggling with the emotions of my own sorrow for Karim and his family on the one hand and with this deep embarrassment on the other. My heart pounded. The hostility was reaching through my protection. It was all I could do to keep seated for the appropriate amount of time until I could stand, make my goodbyes and walk out of the room. Finally when I did leave I felt every eye in the household staring at me.

In my car I sat for a moment at the wheel, trying to collect myself. I had obeyed, but the cost was high. Certainly I would prefer to have remained at home rather than walk right straight into the maw of this open anger.

If I thought I would have to walk through this valley only once I was wrong. A few weeks later, just as midsummer's heat was beginning to settle over our district, another cousin died. Again, I heard of his death through my household. Again, obeying the Lord's direction, I found myself reluctantly walking into a room full of mourners, to the chilly discord of hate. As an act of will I focused my concern away from myself and toward the one person there who was really bereaved, my cousin's widow. She had a child just going on five, the same age as Mahmud. She looked so forlorn standing by herself at the coffin that I wept for her and for her husband.

And then just as I had done at Karim's funeral, I found myself being propelled toward this desperate woman. As I approached our eyes met, and I saw hesitation cross her tear-stained face. Then, with a look of sudden determination, knowingly going against the will of her family, she extended her hand to me. As I held her brown and shaking hand in my own I wept in silence. We exchanged only one or two words, but my heart was praying fervently that the Holy Spirit would reach into her bereavement and keep His promise, even to this Muslim dear one, "Blessed are they who mourn."

"Thank you, Bilquis, thank you," the widow said in a whisper as at last she released my hand. I embraced her and walked out of the room.

Oddly, there were two more funerals in quick succession. This was quite unusual even for a family of our size. But in each case I was told very clearly, very distinctly, by the Lord to get out of my safe little house and go into the place where I was needed. I was not to do too much talking. I was to let my caring presence be its own witness.

And all the while the Lord was working with me. He had so much to teach me, and He was using these funerals as His classroom.

It was during one of these visits to a family funeral that I discovered the next great secret of staying in His Presence.

At a Muslim funeral no one cooks or eats until the body is buried. This usually amounts to a day's fasting and is really not an ordeal. However, that day, as I sat isolated in the crowded room, I suddenly found that I wanted my usual afternoon tea. It was something, I said to myself, which I simply could not do without.

Finally, unable to control my desire, I stood and mumbled an excuse. I had to wash my hands, I said. I slipped out of the house and down the street to a small cafe. There I had my precious tea and returned to the mourners.

Immediately I felt a strange aloneness, as if a friend had left my side. Of course I knew what it was. The comforting Presence of His Spirit had left me.

"Lord," I said to myself, "what have I done?"

And then I knew. I had told a lie when I was excusing myself.

"But it was only a white lie, Lord," I said. I sensed no comforting from the Spirit. Just a deadness.

"But Lord," I pressed, "I don't have to follow those Muslim mourning practices any more. And besides, I just can't do without my tea. You know that."

No sense of His Spirit.

"But Father," I pressed on, "I couldn't tell them that I went out for tea and cake. That would have hurt them."

No Spirit.

"All right, Father," I said. "I understand. It was wrong for me to lie. I realize that I was seeking the approval of men and that I must live only for Your approval. I am truly sorry, Lord. I hurt You. With Your help I will not do that again."

And with those words His comforting Presence flooded me again, like rain falling on a parched lake bed. I was relaxed. I knew that He was with me.

And that was how I learned to move back into His Presence quickly. Whenever I did not feel His nearness, I knew that I had grieved Him. I would search backwards until I spotted the time *when I last knew His Presence.* Then I would review every act, every word or thought until I discovered where I had gone astray. At that point I would confess my sin and ask His forgiveness.

I learned to do this with increasing boldness. Through these exercises in obedience I learned the beautiful secret of repentance. Repentance, I discoverd, was not **tearful** remorse so much as admitting where I had gone wrong and avowing with His help never to make that mistake in the future. As I realized my own weakness, I could call upon His strength.

It was during this time that I discovered there was no such thing as an innocent white lie. A lie is a lie and is always of Satan, the father of lies. He uses "harmless" white lies to get us started in this insidious habit. Lies pave the way for greater temptations to come. Satan whispers that a white lie is "consideration" for other people. We bend ourselves to the world instead of to Jesus who is the Truth.

Though I learned this lesson at the funeral of a relative, it was the beginning of a new kind of life for me, one where I attempted to weed out all lying. From that day on I would try and catch myself every time I was about to commit a white lie. Once a missionary friend invited me to a gathering which I did not want to attend. I was all set to make the excuse that I had another engagement. A warning signal sounded within me and I stopped myself just in time. Instead, I found that I could be truthful and still not hurt anyone's feeling by simply saying, "I'm very sorry, but I won't be able to be there."

Or, there was the day when I sat down to write a letter to a friend in London and almost automatically began writing that I had been out of town for some time and had not been able to answer his last letter. I stopped, pen poised in midair.

Out of town? I had been here all the time. I crumpled the paper, dropped it into the wastebasket and started again. "Dear Friend: Please forgive me for not answering your wonderful letter sooner. . . ."

Little things, certainly. But I was learning that to be careful in small things made it much easier to handle the larger temptations as they came. Besides, life was so much easier when I didn't have to spend a lot of time contriving.

Slowly, surely, it began to dawn on me that I was trying to live with Christ as my constant companion! Of course, it just wasn't possible to do this. So often I caught myself falling into my old ways! But I kept trying.

And in the process I discovered the practical side of the promise, "But seek ye first the kingdom of God, and his righteousness; and all these things shall be added unto you" (Matthew 6:33, KJV). For, as I made the attempt to put God first, some of my other heartfelt needs were given back to me.

One afternoon Raisham came to my room with a startled expression on her face.

"There's a lady in the drawing room waiting to see you," she said.

"Who is it?" I asked.

"Well, Begum Sahib, if I'm not mistaken it's the mother of Karim."

Surely she must be mistaken! Karim's mother would not be coming here!

I walked downstairs wondering who then it could be. But, as I turned the corner into the drawing room, sure enough there stood the mother of my dead cousin. Hearing my steps she looked up, came over and threw her arms around me.

"Bilquis," Karim's mother said, tears forming in her eyes, "I just had to come personally to tell you something. At first, at the funeral, I didn't see you among all the people. But I need to tell you how much comfort you were. It's . . . I don't know . . . something new. Something warm and special."

And at last I saw why I had not been allowed to speak of Jesus directly to Karim's mother during the time of her crushing bereavement. For that would have been to take advantage of her. Now however the situation was quite different. Gently and softly there in my drawing room I spoke to her about how much Jesus meant to me and how He was slowly and inexorably changing so many of my old imperious ways, replacing them with His warm human personality.

"It's true," Karim's mother said. "You did care. You really wanted to share my sorrow."

It was a short visit but a wonderful one. Encouraging in two directions: First, that another human being had actually noticed a change in me; and second, I hoped that this was the beginning of a break in the family boycott.

It didn't happen quickly though. Every time the phone rang it was one of my missionary friends. So one morning just before Mahmud's sixth birthday, when the phone rang I expected to hear Marie. Instead I heard the friendly voice of the mother of the second cousin who had died.

"Bilquis?"

"Yes."

"Bilquis, I just wanted to say how much I appreciate the help you gave my son's wife. She told me you really spoke to her heart."

How interesting. For I had said little. It was Christ who had done the consoling.

We exchanged a few pleasant words and then hung up.

Once again I could not help but be amazed at how Jesus had done the work through me when I said little or nothing about Him directly. It was my being there, representing His Spirit in this time of need that had been the helper.

Over the weeks a few other family members came for short visits. They'd drop by to see Mahmud on his birthday, bringing him sweets and toys. Ostensibly the reason for their visit was to see the boy. Actually, I knew, it was just a good excuse. They really had come to soften some of the hurt of the boycott. The visits were always strained and short. But they were bright, welcome chinks in the terrible wall that had been raised around me.

Almost a year had passed since I had made the decision to accept Christ's call. How the time was flying! Soon my birthday would be here again. One year since I had given myself to the Lord. And now I was looking forward to my first real celebration of Christmas. I had of course seen Christmas celebrations when I was in Europe. But never had I known what Christmas was like viewed from the heart. I borrowed a creche from the Mitchells. When they came to the house with the little manger scene they also brought a small fir tree, and we all sang, "O Christmas Tree . . . O Christmas Tree . . . ," while Mahmud squealed with delight. The servants put the tree in the drawing room and we all decorated it with paper ribbons.

There was something wrong, however.

Much as I enjoyed these festivities, there wasn't much real meaning in them. I began to wonder if I could celebrate Christmas in a way that expressed the change that had come into my life.

And then an idea came to mind. Why not throw a party for everyone—missionaries, and people from the village, even the sweepers. Immediately I heard the warning voice of my family cautioning me not to make a display of my faith; and I also heard the General's voice warning me that he could no longer give me official protection if I got in trouble. I knew the idea of such a Christmas party would be a threat to many. Yet, after much prayer it seemed to me my Presence was strongest when I began to make plans for the unusual gathering.

So I went ahead on Christmas Day and threw the party which caused such a stir in Wah. The village people arrived early and congregated around the tree in the drawing room. Then the missionaries came. Synnove led everyone in song. And then to my astonishment one of the servants announced that an aunt and some cousins from Rawalpindi had arrived on a drop-in visit!

My heart leaped. How would they react! I need not have worried—they reacted in typical upper class-fashion, I'm afraid. First their jaws dropped, then they quietly retired to another room where they sat alone in strained silence.

I did not want to ignore either group so I spent my time going from room to room. It was like running back and forth from a hot shower to a cold shower.

Finally, perhaps because of my own persistence, a few members of my family began to relax. Some even went into the drawing room and joined the festivities around the tree. By the end of the party they were passing small talk with the Olds and the Mitchells, if not with the sweepers.

The party heralded, I hoped, the start of a different kind of year. Not an easier one, just a different one. Because immediately in front of me lay many confusing crossroads which could lead me into trouble if I took a wrong turn. For along with the smattering of relatives and friends who were now returning, came a different kind of visitor. They were people who were determined to convert me back to the Muslim faith. I had a feeling that there were interested onlookers, anxious to see how I would react to these voices beckoning me back home. Should I keep a discreet silence, or should I really speak my mind?

The answer came to me, again, in terms of my Presence. For whenever I tried to be devious I felt uncomfortable and alone. But whenever I answered the loaded questions forthrightly and in love, then I felt that the Lord Himself was right with me.

One afternoon, for instance, there was a soft knock on my door. I was surprised, for it was two o'clock in the afternoon.

"Yes?" The door opened. It was Raisham. "Begum Sahib, you have a visitor."

There was a hesitancy in her soft voice. I had told Raisham that I preferred not to be bothered between noon and three in the afternoon. It was not an order however. A year ago I would have ordered Raisham sharply not to bother me for any reason between noon and three. Now I explained to her that I no longer considered time as something I owned; it belonged to the Lord. If something came up which she herself thought I should see to, then of course she was to come to my room no matter what the hour.

"Begum Sahib, the man is an Englishman." There was a glint of amusement in her brown eyes. "He says he wants to talk about God."

"All right," I said, wondering. "I'll be right down."

Waiting for me in the drawing room was a pale, sandy-haired Englishman. I was interested in noting that he wore typical Pakistani clothes, a white shirt and baggy trousers. With his pale face and white clothes he almost blended into the white walls of my drawing room. After apologizing for dropping in without an appointment, he came to the point.

He said that he had travelled all the way from Karachi to see me; since he had converted from Christianity to Islam, members of my family thought we had interests in common. "Ah," I said to myself, "now I understand. Knowing how much I like the British, they think I will be impressed by an Englishman who has left his Christianity for Islam."

My visitor hemmed and hawed and launched into the purpose of his visit.

"Begum," the man said, "one thing really disturbs me about Muslims who convert to Christianity. It is the Bible. We all know that the Christian New Testament has been changed from what God gave."

He was expressing Islam's main charge against the Bible, that it had been so altered that today's version is untrustworthy. The original, Muslims claim, had agreed with the Koran.

"I hope you won't think I'm being facetious," I said. "I really do want to know something. I've heard often that the Bible was changed but I've never been able to learn who changed it. When were the changes made and what passages were corrupted?"

My visitor leaned back and looked up to the carved ceiling beams, his fingers drumming the arm of his chair. He did not answer. It was unfair of me I guess. As far as I knew there were no answers to these questions.

"You see," I went on, drawing on research I had made, "in the British Museum there are ancient versions of the Bible which were published nearly three hundred years before Muhammad was born. On every issue between Christianity and Islam these old manuscripts are identical with today's Bible. The experts say that in every basic essential today's Bible has not been changed from the original. This is important for me personally. For, to me the Bible has become an alive Word. It speaks to my soul and feeds me. It helps guide me. . . ."

My visitor got to his feet in the middle of my sentence.

". . . and so," I went on, "I find it quite important to

know if there really are places where I'm fooling myself. Can you tell me?"

"You talk about the 'Word' almost as if it were living," my visitor said.

"I believe that Christ is living, if that's what you mean," I said. "The Koran itself says that Christ was the Word of God. I would love to talk with you about it sometime."

"I must be going."

And that was that. I saw my visitor to the door and invited him back. He never did return but others came, some well primed for battle and with such misconceptions! I'll never forget the man who accused Christians of worshipping three separate Gods.

"Your so-called Trinity consists of God, Mary, and Jesus!" he said. "You Christians say that God took a wife who was Mary and from their union Jesus was born. Allah can't have a wife!" he laughed.

I prayed quickly. And a clear line of thought came to mind.

"Do you read the Koran?" I asked.

"Of course."

"Well then, do you remember how the Koran says that Christ was given the Spirit of God?" I had often wondered how the Koran could have such marvelous truths as this. "You perhaps have heard of Sadhu Sundar Singh, the devout Sikh to whom Jesus appeared in a vision. This is how Jesus explained the Trinity to him: 'Just as in the sun there are both heat and light, but the light is not heat and the heat is not light, but both are one, though in their manifestation they have different forms, so I and the Holy Spirit, proceeding from the Father, bring light and heat to the world. . . . Yet We are not three but One, just as the sun is but one.'"

It was quiet in the room when I finished. My guest was deep in thought. Finally he arose, thanked me for giving him time and silently left the house.

As I watched his forlorn figure walk down the graveled driveway it occurred to me to wonder whether my little visits with people like the Englishman and this zealot were really being used by the Lord. I had no way of knowing, for I never heard from either of them again. It didn't matter. I perhaps should not even wonder about results. The only thing that did matter to me was obedience. If the Lord asked me to talk to these people, then that is what I should do.

As the winter rolled into spring, the Lord seemed to give me other ways of speaking too. I went to Lahore and—after a good but strangely uncommunicating visit with my son Khalid—I purchased a hundred copies of the Bible to give away to anyone who was interested. I also bought a quantity of Christian tracts. I gave them away at every opportunity, even leaving them in public restrooms. I'm not at all sure this did any good. Once, when I went back to the restroom, I found my little stack had dwindled but then I looked in the wastebasket. There, crumpled up, were the copies of my tracts.

"It seems so pointless, Lord," I said. "Am I doing what You want? Why is it, Lord," I said raising my hands to my waist in supplication, "that not one single time have I been able to see the results of talking about You?" There was the English convert to Islam, and the General, and all the servants who had fled, and the hundreds of times I had talked with members of my family and with friends—not one of these times bore visible fruit. "It's so puzzling, Lord! I just don't understand why You aren't using me."

As I prayed the sensation of Christ's Presence grew ever stronger in that room. He seemed to fill the atmosphere with strength and comfort. I heard in my heart the distinct suggestion, "Bilquis, I have only one question to ask you. Think back over those times when you have talked with your friends, and with your family. Think back over the times you have accepted people who have come to argue. Have you felt My Presence during those visits?"

"Yes Lord. Yes indeed I have."

"My glory was there?"

"Yes Lord."

"Then that's all you need. It is so often this way with friends. And family. The results are not your problem. All you have to worry about is obedience. Seek My Presence, not results."

So I continued on my course. The odd thing is that it became an increasingly stimulating and invigorating time. Once the Lord had taken my eyes off the "results" and turned them to His Presence, I could enjoy meeting friend after friend, relative after relative without the slightest feeling of frustration. I learned to take advantage of opportunities. Whether the conversation was on politics or clothes, I would ask God to prompt a question which would give me an opening. For example, once when I was talking to a niece, the conversation drifted to my former husband, who was now Pakistan's ambassador to Japan.

"What if Khalid came to your house?" she smiled, lifting an eyebrow.

I looked at her directly. "I would welcome him. I would serve him tea." My niece looked at me incredulously. "I have forgiven him," I continued. "And I hope that he has forgiven *me* for all that I did which hurt him."

"How can you forgive that way!" My niece knew that the breakup had been most difficult.

I explained that I certainly could not forgive in my own strength. I had asked Jesus to help me. "You know," I said, "Jesus invited us all to come to Him with our burdens. Jesus took my burden of hate from me."

My niece sat quietly for a while. "Well," she said, "that is a Christianity I have not heard about. If you're going to talk like that I'll be one of the first to come and learn about your Jesus."

Even here I was disappointed. I had high hopes. I believed that indeed my niece might return to the subject but she never did.

I did have times when the glory left me during this period. It always occurred in the same fashion. I would slip into Satan's trap of convincing me that I sounded pretty good! My arguments were really quite profound!

One day for instance a friend asked me, "Why do you have to be so exclusive? You'll have to admit that we all worship the same God, whether Christian, Muslim, Hindu, Buddhist or Jew. We may call Him by different names and approach Him from different directions, but in the end it's the same God."

"You mean He is like a mountain top to which different paths lead?"

He settled back balancing his cup of tea and nodded. And then I flew to the attack.

"Well," I said, "He may be a mountain top but there is only one path to Him, through Jesus Christ. The Lord said: 'I am the way, the truth and the life.' Not just *a* way," I added sharply, "but *the* way."

My friend put down his cup of tea, grimaced and shook his head. "Bilquis," he said, "did anyone ever tell you that you still come across as haughty?"

And instantly I knew that the man sitting in front of me was speaking for God. My arguments were right. They were Biblical and sound. But the Spirit had left. *Bilquis* was right. *Bilquis* was stating truth. Quickly I said a prayer of repentance and asked the Lord to take over.

"I'm sorry," I laughed. "If I come across as smug because I'm a Christian, then I'm not acting as Christ would want. The more I learn about Christ the more I need correcting. The Lord has so much to teach me and I know He is speaking right now through you."

My visitor left, perhaps closer to the Lord, perhaps not. I doubt that I shall ever know. But I do know that I was, step by painful step, learning to listen and to obey.

And then one night I had another one of those frightening experiences which came only after I had become a Christian. I was in my room preparing for bed when I suddenly felt a powerful presence of evil at my bedroom window. Instantly my mind turned to my Protector and I was warned from going near the window. I dropped to the floor in prayer, asking my Lord to cover me as a mother hen covers her chicks and I felt the strong cloak of His protection. When I arose, the presence at the window was gone.

The next morning, I drove over to the Mitchells. The sun shone brightly on their street but I was still shaking inside. Yet, as I walked up to their door, I felt hesitant about mentioning what happened to me for fear they wouldn't understand.

At the door, Synnove hugged me, then stepped back, her blue eyes questioning me.

"What's wrong, Bilquis?" she asked.

"Well," I ventured, "why do frightening things keep happening after one becomes a Christian?"

She ushered me into the living room where we sat down.

"I don't really know what you mean," she said puzzled. "Has someone threatened you?"

"Not someone," I answered, "*something.*"

"Oh?" she said, and arose and got her Bible. "Here," she said, sitting down and flipping through its pages, "in Ephesians 6 it speaks about that kind of thing." She read: *"We are up against the unseen power that controls this dark world, and spiritual agents from the very headquarters of evil."*

She looked up at me.

"That must be it," I said telling her something about what happened that night.

She listened thoughtfully, and then said, "Why don't you talk to the Olds about it?"

"Well," I said, giving a nervous laugh, "I don't know if I want to even *talk* about it any more."

And that's how I felt at the beginning of our get-together with the Olds that evening. I decided not to bring it up. I'd simply make a fool of myself, I thought. It was probably just my imagination.

However, as I sat talking with Marie Old on a sofa before the fire, I couldn't help mentioning it. I tried to sound light-hearted.

"The strangest thing happened to me last night, Marie," I said. "I had the most frightening experience and I can't explain it."

Her husband, Ken, in his usual relaxed manner, had been sitting in a window seat behind us reading a book. Hearing me, he laid his book down, looked up and sensing my reluctance to talk about it, he, in his own quiet way, gently drew me into explaining the whole episode.

When I finished, I tried to laugh. "And then again," I said lightly, "I may have had too much curry at dinner last evening!"

"Don't minimize the things the Lord will bring you through," he said quietly. "Supernatural things *do* happen." He walked around the sofa and sat in a chair facing us. His face was serious.

He explained the supernatural presence of evil and how God can allow it to come upon a person as a test. As an example, Ken pointed out in the Old Testament how God permitted Satan to attack Job and how He allowed the Evil One to tempt Christ in the wilderness. Both of these, Ken pointed out, were tests. And in each case, he added, Satan's intended victim emerged victorious because of his outspoken faith in God. I couldn't help remembering the attack I suffered the second night before my baptism.

Slowly, the learning continued. But what I did not know as I gratefully considered Ken's comforting teaching, was that the Lord had already started a process which was to leave me more and more alone, yet not lonely; more and more cut off from my family, yet part of a great, supportive family; more and more cut off from the roots which meant so much to me in Wah, yet with deepening roots in a new City.

It was because of these upcoming tests of endurance that He had been placing me, time after time, in situations where I had to depend solely on Him.

11.

Winds of Change

The weaning process began one Sunday a few weeks later, during our regular prayer meeting. I thought that both the Olds and the Mitchells seemed unusually somber that evening.

"What's wrong?" I asked as we walked into the Olds' drawing room. Ken leaned his head back and stared at the ceiling.

"Marie and I are leaving on a year's furlough," he said abruptly.

My first reaction was panic at the thought of abandonment. What would I ever do without the Olds! Of course I would still have the Mitchells, but I depended on both families, together, to be my support. The Mitchells had brought me into my first contact with the church; the Olds had walked closely with me. Was this just a beginning? How long before I lost both families?

Marie must have read my heart. For she stepped over and took my hand. Tears filled her eyes as she spoke.

"My dear," Marie said, "you must realize that it will always be this way. Those we love will always be leaving. Only Jesus stays with you forever."

Ken now joined his wife at my side.

"There's another thing, Bilquis," Ken said. "You can be sure the Lord never leads you out of a safe situation unless He has a purpose. Because of that, you can start rejoicing now, even in the midst of the hurt."

We had only a few weeks more together, the Olds, the Mitchells and I. The departure date grew closer, carrying with it a sense of doom. We all tried to be faith-filled about the vacuum that would be created by Ken's and Marie's leaving but it was play-acting, not at all real.

It was a sad day when the Mitchells and I and others in our small Christian group went to the Olds' house for a goodbye send-off. We did our best even at this last moment to make it a celebration, but our hearts were heavy. We tried to see the moment as a chance not to "let them go" but to "send them out."

It was a brave show. But in our hearts, as we saw the Olds' heavily-loaded automobile lumber off toward the Grand Trunk Road, it seemed to us all that life could never again be as rich.

As I drove back to my own home that day I had a strange sensation of being on my own, now, alone in a hostile community. How ridiculous. The Mitchells were still in Wah, after all!

The weaning process took a new and unexpected turn late one morning, some months after the Olds left, when Dr. Daniel Baksh phoned me. He said he and Dr. Stanley Mooneyham, representing a group called World Vision, headquartered in California, U.S.A., would like to visit me. I had never heard of his organization but my doors were open to anyone, even people who were curious to see what a Muslim-turned-Christian looked like.

Both arrived a few days later. When we finished dinner, Dr. Mooneyham began to speak and it was clear that he was no curiosity-seeker. He was interested in my conversion, all right, but I sensed that he would have been equally interested in the conversion of my gardener. As we sipped tea, he came to the point.

"Will you come to Singapore, Madame Sheikh," Dr. Mooneyham asked, "to testify for the Lord?"

"Singapore?"

"Billy Graham is arranging a large conference there called *Christ Seeks Asia*. It will be for Asiatic Christians of all kinds—Indonesians, Japanese, Indians, Koreans, Chinese, Pakistanis. Your testimony will be an inspiration to us."

It didn't sound right. I had enough to do right there in Wah without taking off for other parts of the world.

"Well," I said, "I'll pray about it."

"Please do!" Dr. Mooneyham said and then shortly he bid me goodbye.

Long after Dr. Mooneyham left, I sat on the veranda thinking and praying, as I had promised, about the invitation. One side of me said that I should take advantage of the opportunity. Another side of me said I should not even think of it.

And then an idea occurred to me.

My passport. Of course. It was just about to expire. It would have to be renewed if I were to go to Singapore. At that time in Pakistan there was much red tape involving passports. The situation was *impossible*. Some people sent their passports in for renewal and *never* got them back.

Why not let this situation act as a voice for the Lord? If He wanted me to go, He would take care of this passport detail.

That very afternoon I filled out the necessary information and posted the passport to the proper officials. As I slipped it in the mail box I had very little doubt that this would be my "No" to the Singapore trip.

A week later an official-looking government envelope came in the mail.

"Hmm," I smiled, "this will be the first step in getting my renewal, some more forms to fill out. And so it will go on for months."

I opened the envelope.

There, all renewed and officially stamped, was my passport.

So it was, a few months later, that I said goodbye to six-year-old Mahmud and drove down to Lahore. There I had a short visit with my son, Khalid, before going on to Karachi where I would board the jet for Singapore. Although it was now 1968 and a year and a half had passed since the Lord met me, Khalid was much like the rest of my family, now showing little interest in my discovery. I suspected that he considered me, at 48, embarked on a strange kind of trip. But I was to be respected as his mother, and we had an enjoyable visit.

Later as I boarded the jet in Karachi and considered the project I was just now undertaking, I had the impression that Khalid was right. What in the world was I doing on this airplane headed for Singapore! There were a lot of Christians aboard and I wasn't too sure I liked what I saw. I shrank from their exuberance. They were singing Gospel songs, shouting back and forth to each other across the aisles, sometimes raising their hands and crying, "Praise the Lord!" I was embarrassed. There was an artificial quality about the joy, not unlike the forced gaiety I had occasionally seen among conventioneers on the streets of London. I found myself muttering that if this was what it meant to travel in Christian circles, I wasn't interested.

What made the moment worse was that, for reasons which I could not define, I felt this trip held a personal significance beyond my safari to Singapore. It was as if the trip were prophetic, foretelling the type of life I would be called upon to lead.

"Oh no, Lord," I said to myself. "You must be playing with me!" Prophetic in what sense? That I was going to have to spend a lot of time among extroverts, traveling in jet airplanes? Back in Wah I was just getting comfortable in my role as a Christian, but that was in a provincial village. There I was in control, at least. Christianity to me was a very private joy, to be shared on my own terms. I definitely did not like the idea of parading myself before hundreds, perhaps thousands of strangers.

As the plane took off I stared out of the window, watching Pakistan fall away below me into the mist. Even though I knew that I would be coming back within just a few days, something warned me that in a very real sense this was a beginning. Although I would return to my home in the physical sense, in another sense I would never come back. This—this group of Christians on an airplane—was my home now.

What could I possibly mean by that! The idea appalled me.

From the Singapore airport we went straight to the conference hall where the meetings were already in progress.

And suddenly, quite to my surprise, I found that I was having a very different reaction to this group of assembled Christians.

There were thousands of men and women in the conference hall, the largest number of people I had ever seen gathered in one place. As I walked into the hall, everyone was singing "How Great Thou Art." I felt the familiar Presence of God's Spirit and had never known it to be so palpitating. Almost instantly I wanted to cry, not out of sadness but out of joy. Never before had I seen such a large crowd of people praising the Lord. I could hardly grasp it. So many people, from so many countries! Different races, different dress! Galleries of praising Christians seeming to rise forever.

Now this was different! Not at all like the group of people on the airplane. I then realized what I had been experiencing on the plane. Everything was suddenly very clear. Those people on the jetliner had been shy, nervous, perhaps even afraid. Afraid of the newness, afraid of flying. They were bluffing and posturing, not in the Spirit in spite of the language. They were no more moving in the Spirit than I was when I scolded one of the servants or reacted violently to an uncle when he tried to pressure me back into Islam. The problem had been their language. Christian talk fooled me. I should have recognized their Christianese as such, covering up a hurting.

But here in this conference center it was different. Socializing was over, worship had begun. If the prophecy I had felt meant being with groups like this, *that* I could appreciate and accept.

One thing still bothered me. Was I really supposed to stand up in front of these thousands of people to talk? It was one thing to speak about my experiences to people I knew personally in Wah. But here? With all these strange-looking people from so many different continents? I did not feel at all safe.

I hurried over to my hotel where I tried to settle down. I looked out the window at teeming Singapore. How different Singapore was from London and Paris. People jostled each other on the streets, hawkers sang their wares and automobiles threaded through the melee, constantly sounding horns. The very press of people seemed to menace me here just as it did in the conference hall. I shuddered, thrust the curtain closed and retreated to the other end of the room where I sat down and tried to calm myself.

"Oh Lord," I cried, "where is Your comforting Spirit?"

And suddenly I recalled a childhood experience of walking with my father through the marketplace in Wah. Father cautioned me to stay by his side but, always active, I wanted to run off. One day I did. A flower display caught my attention and I ran over to it. Suddenly I realized that my father was not at my side. Panic filled me and I burst into tears. "Oh Father," I said, "come find me and I won't ever run away from you again!" Even as I spoke, there he was, his tall slender figure coming quickly toward me through the crowd. I was with him again! All I wanted now was to stay by his side.

As I sat in the hotel room, I realized that in fact I had left my heavenly Father again. By allowing myself to become anxious, I had run off from His comforting Presence. When would I learn that I cannot worry and trust God at the same time! I relaxed in my chair and felt at peace again.

"Oh thank You, Father," I said weeping in relief. "Please forgive me for stepping away from You. You are here, You are in that hall. I'll be safe."

A few minutes later in the hotel lobby, I felt a hand on my arm and heard a familiar voice. I looked around to see Dr. Mooneyham.

"Madame Sheikh, so good to have you here!" Dr. Mooneyham seemed happy enough to see me. "Are you still willing to speak?" It was as if he had been reading my mind.

"Don't worry about me," I said, smiling. "I'll be fine. The Lord is here."

Dr. Mooneyham just stood there, studying my face, as if making a decision about how to interpret my words. After all, I had been using Christianese too, and he wasn't going to take it at face value, possibly let it fool him as it had fooled me on the airplane. Dr. Mooneyham's eyes were reading my very soul. Then suddenly he seemed satisfied.

"Good," he said abruptly. "You're slated for tomorrow morning." He looked at his watch. "You'll have lots of prayer support."

Dr. Mooneyham had understood me correctly. The sense of security lasted through the next morning too, when indeed I did get up in front of those thousands of people gathered in the auditorium to speak of the way the Lord had found me in such a strange way. It was not at all difficult speaking. He was with me as I stumbled and fumbled my way through the talk, embracing me and encouraging me, assuring me that *He* was doing the communicating and not I. And as people surrounded me in loving fellowship after my talk, it was as if I had taken the first step in a new kind of work for the Lord.

The Lord also arranged my meeting a man who would become very important in my life, though I didn't realize it at the time. I was introduced to Dr. Christy Wilson, a kind gentleman who was pastor of a church in Kabul, Afghanistan, which ministered to foreign nationals. We found a rapport in the Lord's Spirit as we discussed his work.

Then, the meetings were over and I was on my way back to Wah. Once again I sensed that the whole trip had a strangely foretelling character, as if God had asked me to come with Him to Singapore so that I could learn more about a type of work He wanted me to do.

Well, I said to myself, at least I'll be headquartered in Wah. Perhaps I wouldn't mind *too* much, going out on an occasional trip from my comfortable and secure ancestral home.

But as the car turned off the Grand Trunk Road toward our house in the trees, I had no way of knowing that the weaning process was going to shatter more of that security.

12.

A Time for Sowing

The next separation step came in the sad news that the Mitchells were leaving on furlough. It would be some time before they would return to Pakistan.

It was more than a year after Singapore. I was sitting in the Mitchells' living room with our small band of Christian professional men and women from the area. It was a sad occasion, the final get-together before David and Synnove left. I could not help thinking of the first time I had come to this same low-verandaed house as a hesitant seeker. So much had happened since then. I looked at the faces of these two who had been so close to me in my introduction to Christ: tall David, his hair graying, and earnest Synnove who had prayed for me so consistently.

"I'm going to miss you terribly, you know that," I said as we all stood on the small lawn in front of the Mitchells' house. "How will I ever get along without your fellowship!"

"Maybe the Lord is teaching you to get along without it," said Synnove. "He's always stretching us, you know, Bilquis, until we don't have a safe handhold left except Him."

It sounded good, but I still didn't like being stretched and told Synnove as much. She just laughed. "Of course

131

you don't, dear Bilquis. Who ever wants to leave the safety of a womb. But adventure lies ahead!"

Synnove got into their old car and closed the door. One more embrace through the window and suddenly the Mitchells' car was rolling dustily away, away from the forlorn whitewashed buildings that had been officers' quarters during the war. Their car disappeared around the corner. Adventure, indeed! Here I was a lonesome Christian in a Muslim town. Would I be able to make it alone?

Several weeks passed, during which time, frankly, it was hard for me to sense the adventure Synnove promised, or the direction and purpose that Ken Old had foretold when he and Marie left what semed such a long time ago. The Sunday evening meeting of Christians continued, first in one home then in another of the five of us who were left, but without the leadership of the Olds and Mitchells the meetings seemed to flounder.

Then one night after a listless meeting an idea struck me. Were we making a mistake trying to do things exactly as the Mitchells and the Olds had done? Our little group was surely going to atrophy if we didn't get some new blood in our midst. What would happen—and I felt my pulse quicken just at the thought—what would happen if we asked people to join the fellowship who were not professionals—not doctors and engineers and missionaries? Suppose we asked Christians and non-Christians alike, the sweepers, the lower classes, to join in fellowship. Perhaps in my own home since it was large and convenient. When I suggested the idea to our fellowship there was some initial resistance, then skeptical agreement. We decided to go ahead. Through direct invitations and through the grapevine also, I passed word along that a Christian evening would be held at my house Sunday night.

I was surprised at how many people turned up. Most were from Rawalpindi where word had travelled. And, just as I hoped, not all were Christians either. Many were simply hungry to find out more about the Christian God.

With those of us from the original group as leaders, we sang and prayed and tried to do what we could to minister to the individual needs of the maids and day laborers and school teachers and business people who also came to the house.

Soon there was a fresh feeling to the Sunday fellowship. The responsibility was awesome. I and the others who were leaders in this small group spent hours on our knees, hours close to the Lord and the Word, trying to be sure that in no smallest way did we diverge from the direction He wished us to take. All of a sudden the "resultless" period I had been experiencing was reversed. I was able to see actual conversions. The first to come to the Lord was a young widow. She cried her hurt and lonesomeness out and then asked the Lord in. It was extraordinary to see the transformation in her personality, from a gloomy, defenseless creature to a hope-filled child of God. Shortly a mechanic from a nearby garage came into the Lord's Kingdom, then a file clerk, then a sweeper.

And all in my own home. I felt honored indeed, although I kept wondering when I would start to hear from the family about this smudge on our reputation. But no one complained. Not yet, anyhow. It was as if the family didn't want to admit what was happening. One day I tripped on a tile in my terrace, fell and suffered a slight bone fracture. My family didn't come; they telephoned instead. But at least they were telephoning!

If opposition to my slowly evolving Christian life was lessening from my family, it was still coming from within me at times. I was yet a very private person, possessive, counting my land and garden my own.

Across the lawn from my house is a road leading to the servants' quarters. Growing next to this road is a tree called the ber, which has a red fruit similar to the cherry. That summer after the Mitchells left, children from the village (perhaps encouraged by reports of a change in my personality) began coming right onto my property to climb the ber and help themselves to its fruit. The intrusion was bad enough, but when their shouts and squeals interrupted my rest time, I leaned out of my window and ordered the gardener to chase the children away. That very day I had the gardener cut the tree down. That would solve the problem permanently!

As soon as the tree was destroyed I realized what I had done. With the tree gone, so was the joy and peace of the Lord's Presence. For a long time I stood in my window staring at the empty place where it had been. How I wished now that the tree were still there so that I could hear the joyful shouts of the children. I realized what the true Bilquis Sheikh was like. All over again I knew that in my own natural self I would never be different. It was only through the Lord, through His grace, that any change could ever take place.

"Oh Lord," I said, "let me come back into Your Presence again please!" There was only one thing to do. Scattered throughout my garden were large trees heavy with summer fruit. The very next day I issued an open invitation to the village children to come and enjoy! And they did too. Even though I'm sure they tried to be careful, branches were broken, flowers trod upon.

"I think I see what You're doing, Lord," I said one afternoon after the children had gone home, and I was surveying the damage. "You found the garden itself to be a place that stood between us. You are weaning me even from the garden! You've taken it away to give to others. But look how they were enjoying it! It's Your garden. I give it up to them with great pleasure. Thank You for using this to bring me back into Your comforting Self."

He did return too. Until, that is, I once again needed a pruning. This time it wasn't the garden, it was my precious rest.

One cold November afternoon I was resting when Mahmud slipped into my room. He was becoming a youth now and his good-humored features foretold a handsome young-man-to-be. But now his face was concerned.

"Mum, there's a woman outside who wants to see you. She's got a baby in her arms."

I lifted my head. "Mahmud," I said, forgetting my own instructions to Nur-jan and Raisham, "You're eight years old now! You *know* that I don't want to see anyone at this time of day."

Mahmud had hardly left the room before the thought struck me: what would the Lord have done? And, of course, I knew what He would have done. He would have gone to the woman immediately, even if it were the middle of the night.

I called to Mahmud, who had not gone far enough down the hall to miss hearing me. Once again he stuck his brown face through the door.

"Mahmud," I said, "what does the woman want?"

"I think her baby is sick," Mahmud said, coming now into the room. I could see the concern in his eyes.

"Well bring her to the reception room then," I directed as I prepared to go downstairs.

In a moment I joined Mahmud, the woman and her child. The woman was dressed in the coarse, baggy clothes of a peasant. She might have been the baby's grandmother. She had a wizened face, shrunken shoulders and her pantaloons bagged around a thin frame. Only when she lifted her face and stared at me with deep brown eyes could I see that she herself was little more than a child.

"What can I do for you?" I asked, my heart melting.

"I heard about you in my village, and I walked here."

The place she mentioned was twelve miles away. No wonder the poor thing looked so tired. I sent servants for tea and sandwiches. I wondered if she were still nursing the baby; in some villages mothers nurse their children up to three years of age. The baby's eyes stared listlessly at the crystal chandelier, its tiny mouth still. I laid hands on the child's forehead to pray for him; it was hot and dry. As I laid hands on the mother's head, I could feel generations of my family wincing. In the old days, I would have been horrified if even this peasant's shadow had fallen on me.

My heart went out to these little ones, the mother and the child, as I asked God for healing in the name of Jesus. When the maid came I told her also to bring some vitamins for the mother. We visited for half an hour, the mother telling me of her life with a husband who had been crippled in an accident, the new baby, not enough food. And indeed she was nursing the baby—it was the cheapest way to feed him. When the mother finally rose to go, I restrained her with a gesture.

"No," I whispered. "Not yet. We must find some way to see to it that you and the baby are taken care of." Immediately as I said this, the old Bilquis Sheikh began to grow nervous. What if word got out to other needy people in Wah that the Begum Sahib in the big garden provided a soft touch? Wouldn't we be swamped with lines of other skinny, emaciated, sickly, desperate people?

But even as my heart whispered this question, I knew that I had no choice. Either I had meant it or I had not meant it when I gave myself *and all that I possessed* to the Lord.

". . . and, of course, your husband needs attention too. Let's get you all to the hospital. And let's get some decent food into your bodies. Then, if your husband still can't find work, let me know."

That's all there was to the visit. I made arrangements for the hospital to bill me and waited. But the woman never returned. I was a little surprised. When I asked the servants if they knew what had happened to her, they—as usual— had the answer. She and the baby and her husband had indeed gone to the hospital, and now they were all better. The husband had work. My ego bridled at first at the ungratefulness of this woman for not returning to give thanks, but the Lord checked me. "Is that why you helped her? So that you could be thanked? I thought thanksgiving was supposed to go to Me!"

And of course He was right. I went back in my mind to the place where I first felt that *I* had taken care of this woman. Then I asked the Lord to forgive me, and never to allow me to fall into that trap again. "Lord," I sighed, "Your arm must be tired from picking me up so often."

It seemed through those days that I would have little moments of success in the job of living close to the Lord, only to be brought back to earth quickly with resounding failure. I wondered if this were the pattern usually followed in the Christian life. Since I had no one to talk to then, I had to carry these questions secretly.

One morning while Nur-jan was administering my toilette a redbird fluttered to the window sill.

"Oh!" I exclaimed, "look at what the Lord has sent us this morning!"

There was silence as Nur-jan quietly went on brushing my hair. I was a bit surprised; Nur-jan was normally so talkative. Then she observed shyly, "Begum Sheikh, do you know that when you start talking of the Lord your whole appearance changes?"

That afternoon I placed an order for several more Bibles at the mission shop in Islamabad. They were a special kind of Bible, designed for children. I had discovered the usefulness of these Bibles with Mahmud. I discovered also that the servants around the house were picking up the brightly illustrated little book. When the Bibles arrived, I made a special point of giving one to Nur-jan. Imagine my joy when one day she came to speak to me privately.

"Begum Sahib," Nur-jan said, her plump face full of emotion, "I have something to tell you. Do you remember how you have so often told us that if we want to know this Jesus, all we have to do is ask Him to come into our heart?" At this she broke into tears. "Well I did, Begum Sahib.

And He did come in. I have never felt such love, ever, in my whole life!"

I couldn't believe my ears. I threw my arms about the girl and embraced her. We danced a little crying waltz around the bedroom.

"What an incredible piece of news, Nur-jan. Now we are three Christians—you and Raisham and I. We must celebrate!"

So Raisham and Nur-jan and I all had tea together. It wasn't the first time I had drunk tea with people of the serving class. But it still gave me a slight shock. As the three of us Christians daintily sipped our drinks and nibbled at our cake together, chatting like old friends, I found my mind wandering. What had happened to the woman who had retreated to this same estate, to hide from wealthy society? Here she was, sitting with the maids. How my family and friends would be scandalized. How my old friends and family would wonder! I thought back to the way I used to vent my frustrations in sharp orders and outbursts of temper. If I noticed dust on a chair rung, if the servants chatted too loudly in the kitchen, if my lunch were delayed a moment, the whole household could depend on an outburst. The Lord had really been working with me, and I felt His company with great satisfaction.

It was not that I wanted to become a saint. But I was beginning to learn that my responsibility of being a representative of Jesus Christ would not allow me to do anything that would dishonor His Name. And He was also teaching me that one's actions spoke louder than words when it came to witnessing for Christ.

But then I noticed a strange thing at our evening meetings. Nur-jan was not among the dozen villagers who were now joining us in my drawing room. How odd! One day after she had done my hair I asked her to stay behind for a moment. Wouldn't she like, I said, to join us this Sunday?

"But Begum," Nur-jan said, startled, her face whitening, "I just cannot talk about what happened to me, or go to a meeting. My husband is a devout Muslim. We have four children. If I say that I have become a Christian he will just turn me out."

"But you *have* to declare your faith," I insisted. "There is no other way."

Nur-jan stared at me unhappily, then left the room, shaking her head and mumbling. I could just barely make out the words, "But it can't be done."

A few days later I was visiting the Reverend Mother Ruth whom I had also come to know at the Holy Family Hospital. I always enjoyed talking to her. The Reverend Mother mentioned how many people in Pakistan are secret believers.

"Secret believers!" I exclaimed. "I do not see how that is possible. If you are a Christian why aren't you shouting the news!"

"Well," said Mother Ruth, "look at Nicodemus."

"Nicodemus?"

"He was a secret believer. Check chapter three of the Gospel of John."

I opened my Bible then and there and began to read how this Pharisee came to Jesus late one night to find out more about His kingdom. I had often read this stirring chapter but not until then did I realize that of course Nicodemus was a secret believer.

"Perhaps at a later date Nicodemus expressed his belief openly," the Sister said. "But as far as the Scriptures show, he was careful not to let his fellow Pharisees know."

The next day I called Nur-jan into my room and read the verses about Nicodemus to her. "I'm sorry I made you uncomfortable," I said. "In time the Lord may show you how to declare your faith. In the meanwhile, just listen carefully to His leading."

Her face brightened. Later I watched her humming happily at her work. "I hope I did the right thing, Lord," I said. "What I have to watch is that I not set myself up in judgment against anyone."

Just a few days later I discovered for myself, with new intensity, how difficult it was to become a Christian in this part of the world.

One afternoon the phone rang. It was one of my uncles, a relative who had been particularly sharp with me. Even as the family boycott began to thaw slightly, this uncle had never been in touch, never spoken. His voice on the phone was sharp.

"Bilquis?!"

"Yes."

"I hear that you are leading others astray. You are taking them from the true faith."

"Well, dear Uncle, that's a matter of opinion."

I could imagine the man's face getting flushed with the anger that showed in his voice. "It's one thing for you to make these decisions yourself. Quite another for others to follow. You must stop this, Bilquis."

"Uncle, I appreciate your concern but I must remind you that you are to run your life and I will run my own."

The very next day when my new chauffeur was driving me home from a visit with Tooni, a man stood in the road and tried to stop the car. My chauffeur knew that I often stopped for hitchhikers. But he did not want to stop this time.

"Please don't ask me to stop, Begum," he said in a determined voice. He swerved around the man, his tires squealing on the edge of the highway.

"What do you mean?" I leaned forward in the seat. "You don't think that man was trying to . . . ?"

"Begum . . ."

"Yes?"

"Begum, it's just that . . ." the man lapsed into silence and all my questioning could not drag any further information out of him.

But it was just a week later that another one of my

servants slipped into my room minutes after I had retired for my afternoon rest.

She closed the door behind her.

"I hope you will not mind," she said in a low whisper. "But I simply must warn you. My brother was in the mosque in Rawalpindi yesterday. A group of young men began talking about the damage you are doing. They kept saying something would have to be done. Soon. To shut you up."

The girl's voice was shaking.

"Oh Begum Sahib," she said, "must you be so open? We are afraid for you and for the boy."

My heart skipped. Now it was my turn to wonder whether it had not been best to remain a secret believer in this land, and yes, even in this family where Jesus was anathema.

13.

Storm Warnings

Two months passed after the report of threats against me. Nothing occurred more threatening than hostile glances from a few young men, and I began to wonder if the alarms were groundless.

Now it was Christmastime again, a few years after I had found the Babe of Bethlehem. Even though some family members had been visiting me, the warning phone call from my uncle reminded me that relationships within my family were still strained and I felt it would be a good idea to have a dinner party for my relatives and friends, to see if now we could do something further to heal the breach.

So I spent considerable time making up a guest list. Then one evening, before going to bed, I slipped that list into my Bible for safekeeping, intending to have the invitations sent out the next morning.

But that was never to take place.

For when I opened the Bible the next morning to take out the list my eyes fell on a passage. Incredibly, it read:

> *When you give a luncheon or a dinner party, don't invite your friends or your brothers or relations or wealthy neighbors, for the chances are they will invite you back, and you will be fully repaid. No, when you give a party, invite the poor, the lame, the crippled and the blind.*

That way lies real happiness for you. They have no means of repaying you, but you will be repaid when good men are rewarded—at the resurrection.

Luke 14:12

"Lord, is that Your word for me?" I wondered, holding the Bible in one hand and the guest list in the other. Sure enough, most of my relatives and neighbors and friends were well-to-do. I had told myself this was an opportunity to get Muslim and Christian together, but actually I saw that pride had been showing through. I wanted to demonstrate to my family that I still had friends among the wealthy class.

I crumpled up the list.

Instead, I did exactly what the Bible said. I made up a list of widows, orphans, unemployed and poor people of the village and then invited all of them to attend Christmas dinner. This included everyone, even all the beggars. I made some of the invitations myself, others I passed along through my own staff. News like this travels fast and soon my servants were bringing back word that the whole village was planning to come. For a moment I had misgivings. All those *people*. I thought of the pair of silk handmade Persian rugs I had recently ordered for the living room. Oh well, I thought, I could put the good things up out of the way during that time.

So we started preparations. Mahmud's eight-year-old enthusiasm was infectious as he helped me gather presents for the people who would come. We found woolen shirts for the boys, brightly colored garments for the young girls, rolls of red, pink and purple cloth for the women, warm pantaloons for the men, wraps and shoes for the children. The servants and I spent hours wrapping the gifts, tying the packages with silver ribbons.

One day there was a knock on the door. A group of womenfolk from Wah were standing outside. They wanted to help. "Not for pay, Begum," their spokesman explained. "We just want to help you put on the dinner."

Suddenly the whole celebration had become a community affair. For decoration, I asked a family of potters in the village to make lamps, the small oil pottery lamps still commonly used in that part of Pakistan. I ordered 500 of them. I had the village women come to the house, where we made wicks by twisting cotton into strands. As we worked, natural opportunities arose to talk about Christ. As we placed the lamps around the house, for instance, I told the story about the wise and foolish virgins.

The food was another exciting project. Again the village women helped me prepare typical Pakistani sweets and sliced almonds and the delicious legus nuts. They pounded silver paper into strips so thin we could stick them on the sweetmeats as a colorful foil.

The village people began to arrive at the house on December the 24th and continued coming for what turned out to be a week's festival. How beautiful all the lamps were decorating every cranny, sitting cheerily along rails and sills. Mahmud had a wonderful time playing with the village children. I had never seen these children's eyes sparkle so, nor, for that matter, Mahmud's. Squealing and laughing filled the house. From time to time Mahmud would come to me with requests.

"Mum," he would say, "there are five more boys standing outside; can they come in?"

"Of course," I laughed, patting him on the back and feeling sure that there were more children in our house right now than lived in all of Wah. When I talked with the villagers about how Christ had instructed us to treat each other in this way their response was, "Did He *really* walk with people like us?"

"Yes," I said, "and today what we do for others, we do for Him."

Finally, after the festivities were over and I was able to slump down in a chair without worrying about sitting on a sleeping child, I sighed in contentment to God. "Is this what You wanted me to do?" And I seemed to hear the soft response: "Yes." And then I noticed: I had forgotten to put up the new Persian rugs. Yet they seemed none the worse for wear.

Many of the poor never forgot that party. About a month later, I heard through one of the servants about a funeral in Wah. The wife of the local *mullah* complained loudly that I had made a mistake losing my faith. Someone else, however, replied: "Have you seen the Begum Sahib lately? Have you done any of the things she has done since she became a Christian? If you want to learn anything about God, why don't you go see her?"

But there was another side to this experience too. For I learned that there were forces in Wah which did not take kindly to the party.

"Begum Sahib," an old retainer who worked in our garden stopped me one day. He touched his forehead. "A minute please?"

"Of course."

"Begum Sahib Gi, there is talk in the town that you should know about. One speaks about how the Begum has become a problem. There are those in the village who say they will have to do something about you."

"*About* me?" I said. "I don't understand."

"Neither do I, Begum Sahib. But I just feel you should know. . . ."

Warnings like this, sometimes coming close together, sometimes spread months apart, began to occur with increasing regularity over the next year. It was almost as if the Father were trying to prepare me for a difficult time to come.

One day, for instance, three small boys came to our house from the village. Later I wondered if they were God's messengers, arriving in these little forms. For Mahmud came to me with news from the boys. He was shivering and his eyes were wide with fear.

"Mum, do you know what my friends said? They said

that in the village people were planning to kill you. They will do it after Friday prayers." He began sobbing. "If you die, I will kill myself!"

What was I to do! I gathered Mahmud's eight-year-old form in my arms, stroked his tousled black hair and tried to comfort him. "My dear child," I said, "let me tell you a story." And I recounted to him the tale of Jesus' first sermon in Nazareth, when the crowd became so angry and determined to stone Him. "Mahmud," I said, "Jesus passed through the midst of them. There wasn't a thing anyone could do to Jesus until and unless the Father allowed it to happen. The same is true with you and me. We have His perfect protection. Do you believe that?"

"Do you mean we will never be hurt or harmed?"

"No, I don't mean that. Jesus was hurt. But only when His time had come to suffer. We do not need to live a life of constant fear that something terrible will happen to us. For it cannot happen to us until our moment has come. And maybe that will never happen. We will simply have to wait and see. But in the meantime we can live in great confidence. Do you understand?"

Mahmud looked at me and his brown eyes softened. Suddenly he smiled, wheeled on the spot and ran off to play, shouting happily. It was the best answer to my question he could possibly have given.

I wish I could say that I myself felt as confident. Not that I disbelieved what I had said to Mahmud. It was that my faith was not yet childlike. I rose and carried my Bible out into the garden. My heart was not exactly light. How dare they try to force me from my land!

The fall weather was crisp and dry; as I slowly walked along the graveled path, I could hear a fish splash in my little stream and the far-off call of a bird. Chrysanthemums and other summer leftovers cheered the path. I breathed the pleasant sparkling air. This was my land, and my people. This was my country. My family had served it well for seven hundred years. This was my home, and I could not, *would not* leave it!

Yet events were taking place which were totally out of my control, and which did not bode well for my stubborn determination to stay in my home.

In December of 1970, four years after my conversion, Pakistan had its first national one-man-one-vote election. It looked as if the People's Party would carry the day. And that was not exactly good news for me. For none of my highly placed friends were also friends of this party. "Islam our Faith, Democracy our Policy, Socialism our Economy" was the new party's slogan. It was a slogan designed to appeal to the man on the street. I know that the common ordinary Pakistani felt a new sense of power. Was this good for me? Probably it was good for the new Bilquis, but there was an inherent danger too. For nothing fires the zeal of a fanatic more than the belief that his government will back him in his exploits. My old reputation was certainly not that of a democrat; socialism did not fit the age-old traditions of our family; and Islam?—well, now I was a traitor.

I followed the events somewhat from a distance. One day, however, an old government friend of my father's from Sardar arrived. Despite his despair over my new faith, he had tried to stay close to me. From time to time he would call or visit just to make sure that everything was all right.

Now he sat with me on the white silk-covered divan in our drawing room, sipping tea.

"Bilquis," he said, his voice low, "are you aware of what is happening and how it can affect you?"

"Do you mean with the Pakistan People's Party?"

"They won the election of course. How much do you know about Zulfikar Ali Bhutto."

"I knew him well," I said.

"Don't you read the paper? Listen to the radio?"

"No, you know I don't take time for that."

"Well, I advise that you do take time. The government situation has changed. I doubt if you can count on him as you did on previous presidents," he added. "You have, my dear, lost what influence you may have had in high circles. That era is over."

Half an hour later as I waved my old friend out of the driveway and returned to call the maid to clean up, I realized that a strange thing had happened with my old friend's visit. It was as if he had spoken for the Lord, preparing me for the fact that my protective, influential friends were gone, bringing me one more step toward total dependence on the Lord.

It wasn't too long before I began sensing a growing hostility. I saw it in the eyes of men as I walked in Wah. I'll never forget the change in the attitude of a minor official with whom I discussed taxes on my property. In the past he had been a servile man, bowing and touching his forehead. Now the little fellow was openly hostile. It was evident in his clipped remarks and the contemptuous way he slapped the forms down in front of me.

And later as I was strolling along the road outside my house, I glimpsed a man who usually went out of his way to speak to me. Now I noticed something quite different. He caught sight of me, quickly turned his head and began to study the horizon as I passed. Inwardly, I chuckled. "Lord, don't we all behave like children!"

Interestingly, the new government seemed to have little effect upon my household staff. Except for Nur-jan, who was still quietly enjoying her new walk with Jesus, and Raisham, my other Christian servant, my entire staff were faithful followers of Muhammad. Yet a real affection existed between us. More than once my Muslim servants slipped into the bedroom to plead with me. "Please, Begum Sahib Gi," they said in low voices, "if you should have to leave . . . or if you should decide to leave . . . don't worry about us. We'll find work."

What a different relationship I had with my staff now than a short four years before.

Dreams, too, played a remarkable role during that time. Dreams had always been a part of my Christian experience, ever since the day I first met Jesus, who came in a dream to feast at the table with me. Now these strange and mystic experiences, such as Paul said he experienced, became even more active.

One night I found myself taken out in spirit and crossing the ocean at a terrific momentum. Like the speed of light I came to what I felt was New England, though I had never been to America. I came before a house, or was it a nursing home? I floated into a room with twin beds. In one lay a middle-aged woman with a round face, clear blue eyes and a mixture of gray and white short hair. A white embossed cotton spread in a triangular pattern covered the bed. She was obviously very ill; I sensed she had cancer. A nurse sat in a chair reading. And then I saw my Lord in the corner of the room. I kneeled down before Him and asked what I should do.

"Pray for her," He said. So I went to the woman's bed and prayed fervently for her healing.

In the morning I sat at my window still awed by what had happened in that room across the sea. Why did Jesus ask me to pray for the woman? He was right there. Yet He had asked me to pray for her. I was beginning to get a glimmer of a tremendous revelation. Our prayers are vital to our Lord. He works through them. I was led to the fifth chapter of James: *Believing prayer will save the sick man; the Lord will restore him and any sins that he has committed will be forgiven. . . . Tremendous power is made available through a good man's earnest prayer. . . .*

Thus our prayer releases this power into the person for whom we plead.

Another time I envisioned walking up a gangplank as if boarding a ship. The gangplank led into a room. Christ was standing in the room. He seemed to be giving me in-

structions. Then I walked back down the gangplank. At the
end of it a lady was waiting, dressed in western clothes, a
skirt and jacket. She appeared to have been waiting for me.
She came up to me, linked her arm in mine and started to
take me away.

"Where are we going, Lord?" I asked over my shoulder.
But He would not tell me.

The dream seemed to be saying that I would be going
on another trip. Although this time I would be going to an
unknown destination, Jesus would be watching over the
journey. The dream left me in a state of preparedness so
that I was not startled by the news an old friend brought me.

In March 1971, just a few months after Bhutto had taken
office, I had a vist from Yaqub, an old government friend.
He had been close to our family for years. In fact, when
my husband was Minister, there was a time when Pakistan
was in an economic decline with a serious trade imbalance.
Yaqub and I had helped inaugurate a self-help program
which came to be called the *Simple Living Plan*. The basic
idea was to encourage Pakistan industries to produce our
own goods, lessening the need for imports.

We had followed each other around the country helping
small factories and cottage industries get started. We had
encouraged local people to weave fabric and then start
production of clothing. We, ourselves, had voluntarily entered an austerity program, wearing homespun garments.
It was all to the good, for the *Simple Living Plan* was a
success. As local factories began to thrive, the economic
condition of Pakistan improved. Through the years since,
Yaqub would occasionally visit me to discuss politics and
world affairs. He knew a good deal about our family hold-
ings, for he had visited the many estates we had throughout
Pakistan, and he knew that most of our funds were tied up
in real estate.

"Bilquis," he said, in a tone that was apologetic, "some
friends and I have been talking and . . . er, the subject of
your financial health has come up. Have you considered

selling some of your land? I'm not sure how safe it is for you to have all of your funds tied up in real estate, with Bhutto promising land reform."

What a thoughtful thing for Yaqub to do. And not without risk either. With the growing hostility toward the ruling class of yesterday, his government staff car outside my house could easily serve to bring criticism on his own shoulders.

"Thank you, Yaqub," I said, trying to control my voice. "But as things stand now I am determined. Nothing—nothing at all will force me to move out!"

It was an infantile thing to say of course. The old Bilquis with her imperious, stubborn way was showing through. Nonetheless it was an attitude which did not surprise my friend at all. "That's the answer I expected, Bilquis," Yaqub said, stroking his moustache and laughing. "Just the same, the time may come when you may want to leave Pakistan. If you need help . . ."

"If the time does, my good friend, I will be sure to remember your offer."

Another dream: this time from Raisham, usually so reserved.

"Oh Begum Sheikh," my maid cried, kneeling her tall slender form by the divan on which I sat in my bedroom that cold night I met the Lord. "I've had a horrible dream. Can I tell you about it?"

"Of course."

I listened closely. Raisham told me that in her dream some evil men had come into the house and were holding me prisoner. "I fought with them," she cried. "I called out 'Begum, run!' And in the dream I saw you running out of the house and escaping."

The maid's dark brown eyes were moist with tears. It was I who had to comfort her. But for me this was not difficult. In the words which I spoke, I found myself listening to advice which I should take to heart. "My dear," I said, "I have been hearing much from the Lord lately about the possibility of having to flee. And this may occur. I at first refused to believe. But now I am beginning to wonder."

"It is possible," I said, lifting her pale chin upwards and smiling, "that I may have to go. But if I do, it will be in the Lord's timing. I am learning to accept that. Can you believe me?"

The little maid was silent. Then at last she spoke, "What a wonderful way to live, Begum Sahib."

"It is indeed. It is the only way. Nothing, any longer, is in my own control."

And although I did believe everything I said, as the young maid disappeared from my bedroom, I found myself not quite as in charge of my emotions as I may have sounded. Fleeing? Running away? Me?

The series of message "experiences" began to come more rapidly in the autumn of 1971. One day Nur-jan came to me breathless and taut with emotion.

"What is it, Nur-jan?" I said as she started to brush my hair, her hands trembling.

"Oh, Begum Sahib," Nur-jan sobbed, "I don't want you to be hurt."

"Hurt by what?"

Nur-jan dried her eyes. She told me that her brother, her own brother, had been to the mosque the previous day, and that a group of men had said that at last the time had come to take action against me.

"Do you have any idea of what they meant?"

"No, Begum Sahib," Nur-jan said. "But I am afraid. Not only for you but for the boy, too."

"A nine-year-old child? They wouldn't . . ."

"Begum Sahib, this is not the country it was even five years ago," said Nur-jan seriously, so unlike her usually bubbly self. "Please be careful."

And indeed, it wasn't but a few weeks later that it happened.

It had been such a lovely day. Autumn was in the air. The monsoon season was over and the weather was crisp and dry. Nothing untoward had happened for days on end and I found myself saying that after all we were living in a modern age. It was 1971, not 1571. Holy wars were a thing of the past.

I went up to my room for my prayer hour.

But suddenly, without knowing why, I had the strongest urge to get Mahmud and to rush outside to the lawn!

What a foolish thing to do. But the urge was so definite that I dashed down the hall, woke Mahmud up from his siesta, and without explanation hurried the groggy and protesting child down the hall.

Still feeling foolish, I dashed down the stairs, threw open the French doors and ran outside.

The moment I stepped onto the terrace, I smelled acrid smoke. Someone was burning pine boughs. We had a long-standing rule that no one was allowed to burn trash on my land. I went in search of the gardener and when I rounded the side of the house was instantly filled with horror.

There, heaped against the house, was a mound of dried pine boughs, ablaze. The crackling flames, hot and fast, raced up the side of the building, leaping high.

I screamed. The servants came running. Soon some were rushing back and forth to the streams with buckets filled with water. Others had unreeled the garden hose and were spraying the flames but our water pressure was low. For a moment it looked as if the fire was going to catch the timbers which stuck out from the end of the building under the roof. They began to smoke and smoulder. There was no way to throw water that high. The only way we could keep the house from burning down was to quench the flames themselves.

On we raced, against time. The ten servants which were on the staff formed a line to the stream passing buckets of water from one person to another, sloshing it over in their hurry.

On everyone worked for half an hour, until finally the leaping flames began to be brought under control. We stood, about a dozen of us, in a circle around the fire. All of us were perspiring, all of us shaking. In another few minutes the house would have been ablaze, impossible to quench.

I caught Nur-jan's eye. She shrugged ever so slightly and nodded her head.

I knew exactly what she was thinking. The threat had been carried out. I looked at the wooden roof beams, their ends charred black, and the soot stains on the white walls of my house. I thanked the Lord that nothing else had happened and shuddered to think of what could have happened if I had not been directed outside at that very moment.

An hour later, after the police had come to investigate, make their notes, question me and the staff, I was once again seated in my room. I picked up the Bible to see if the Lord had anything special to say to me.

One phrase leaped off the page.

"Haste thee, escape thither; for I cannot do anything till thou be come thither" (Genesis 19:22).

I put the book down and looked up. "All You have to do now is show me the *way* You want me to leave. Will it be easy, or will it be hard?

"And above all, Lord," I said, this time with tears suddenly filling my eyes, "what about the boy? Can he come too? You have been stripping me of everything. Does that include the child as well?"

One day six months later, in May of 1972, the Lord spoke to me still again through another dream. Raisham came to me with worry written in her eyes.

"Begum Sahib," Raisham said, "is the cash box safe?"

She was referring to the portable strong box in which I kept the household cash.

"Of course it's safe," I answered. "Why?"

"Well," Raisham explained, obviously trying to control

her voice, "I had a dream last night in which you were motoring on a long trip. You had the cash box with you."

"Yes?" I said. This wasn't too unusual, since I often carried the cash box with me on trips.

"But the dream was so *real*," Raisham insisted. "And the sad part is that as you were traveling, people stopped you and stole the cash box."

She trembled and once again I had to comfort her with assurance that the loss of my money would lead me into a still closer dependence on God. After she went back to her work I thought about that dream. Could it be prophetic? Could it be telling me that my finances would be taken from me? Would I soon be completely on my own, hurtling into the unknown with no means of support?

These were astonishing days. For just two months later, on a hot July day in 1972, a servant came to announce the arrival of my son Khalid.

"Khalid?" My son still lived in Lahore. Why a special trip, especially in this intense heat? What was so important that it could not be handled on the telephone?

Khalid was waiting for me in the drawing room. "Son!" I exclaimed as I walked in. "How great to see you! But why didn't you phone?"

Khalid came over and kissed me. He closed the drawing room door and, without preamble, he plunged into the purpose for his visit. "Mother, I've heard a frightening rumor." He stopped. I tried to smile. Khalid lowered his voice and went on, "Mother, the government is going to expropriate much private property."

My mind went back to the visit from my government friend who had said the same thing, more than a year earlier, back in March, 1971. Was his prophetic visit coming to pass now? Khalid told me that Bhutto was starting his land reforms and that it was very likely that my properties would be among the first to be nationalized.

"What do you think I should do?" I asked. "Will they take it all or just part?"

Khalid got up from his chair and walked over to the garden window, deep in thought. Turning back to me he said:

"Well, Mother, nobody knows. Perhaps it would be best to sell *some* of your properties in small lots. That way the new owner will be protected from a total government takeover."

The more I thought about it, the more I felt Khalid's suggestion made sense. We drove over to discuss the issue with Tooni, all of us agreeing that this was the right way to proceed. It was decided then. Khalid would go back to Lahore. We would join him there to arrange the paperwork. Tooni, Mahmud and I would follow shortly.

So it was that one hot morning in July of 1972, the three of us found ourselves nearly ready for the drive to Lahore to see real estate agents about my properties. As I stepped out of the house I was struck by the beauty of my garden. Summer blossoms were at their height and even the springs seemed to tinkle louder than usual.

"We'll be back in a few weeks," I said to the assembled staff on the front steps of the house. Everyone seemed to accept the idea. Everyone that is but Nur-jan and Raisham. Nur-jan suddenly burst in tears and rushed away.

Sadly I went up to my bedroom to pick up an item I forgot. When I turned again into the hall to go back downstairs, Raisham was standing in front of me. She took my hand, her eyes wet with tears.

"God go with you, Begum Sahib Gi," she said softly.

"And He with you," I answered.

Raisham and I stood in the hall silently together, saying nothing but understanding everything. Somehow I sensed that I would never see this tall slender person again—she with whom I had become so close. I squeezed her hand and whispered, "There is no one who can do my hair like you."

Raisham put her hands to her face and rushed away from me. I was about to close the bedroom door when something stopped me. I walked back into the room and stood there.

A hush settled over the white-furnished room. The morning sun flooded in from the garden window. This is where I had come to know the Lord.

I turned my back on the room and on my precious garden, where I had so often known the Lord's Presence, and headed outside to the car.

There were people I would be extremely glad to see in Lahore. First, of course, Khalid, his wife and their teenaged daughter. Then there was the possibility of seeing the Olds. I had written that I would be coming to Lahore. Their new mission was in a village some distance from the town, but I hoped that I could see these old friends.

Lahore, as usual in July, was broiling, its ancient streets steamed with rain from the last monsoon. As we threaded our way through the crowded downtown streets, a loudspeaker on a minaret above us crackled, then broke into the metallic voice of a muezzin's noontime prayer. Traffic suddenly lightened as cars and trucks pulled to the curb. Drivers climbed down to the sidewalk, laid out their prayer mats and began prostrating themselves.

Tooni could only stay with us for a very short time because of prior obligations. After we got the necessary paperwork done and had a short visit, Khalid took us to the railroad station so that Tooni could catch her train. It was a poignant moment at the station, more poignant than I could understand. According to plan, Mahmud would be seeing his mother again in just a few days. Yet we all sensed something unusual about the leave-taking. Mahmud, lanky for nearly ten, tried to hold back the tears as he kissed his mother. Tooni cried openly as she embraced the boy. Suddenly I found myself crying too and we all three hugged each other there on the station platform.

Finally, Tooni threw her dark chestnut hair back and laughed: "Oh come on, we're not having a funeral."

I smiled, kissed her again, and Mahmud and I watched her climb aboard the coach. As the engine tooted and the cars slowly began to leave the station, a pang caught my heart. I searched for Tooni's face in the coach window. We located her and both Mahmud and I blew kisses.

Hungrily, I fastened Tooni's face in my mind, etching it in my memory.

The next day I spent time with realty men who advised me that my property sale would take several weeks. Khalid assured us that we would be welcome as long as we wanted to stay.

The one thing that disturbed me was that I would not have spiritual fellowship. I knew now why disciples went out two by two. Christians *need* each other for sustenance and counsel.

I called the Olds. How great it was to hear Marie's voice! We laughed together and cried together and prayed together on the phone. Though their schedule prevented them from coming to Lahore, they could of course put me in touch with Christians in town. Marie mentioned especially a college professor's wife, Peggy Schlorholtz.

Strange! Why did my heart beat faster at the name?

Within minutes, Peggy and I were on the phone with each other. Within hours, she was in Khalid's drawing room. When she saw me her face broke into a smile.

"Tell me, Begum Sheikh," she said, "is it true that you met Jesus for the first time in a dream? How *did* you come to know the Lord?"

So there in the drawing room I told Peggy the whole story, just as it had begun six years before. Peggy listened intently. When I finished she took my hand and said the most amazing thing.

"I wish you would come to America with me!"

I looked at her, dumbfounded. But again my heart was racing.

"I mean it," said Peggy. "I'm leaving soon to put my son in school. I'll be in the States for four months. You could travel with me and speak to our churches there!"

She was so enthusiastic that I did not want to dampen

her spirits. "Well," I said smiling, "I do appreciate your invitation. But let me pray about it."

The next morning a maid brought a note to me. I read it and laughed. It was from Peggy. "Have you prayed yet?" I smiled, crumpled the note and did nothing. It was just too preposterous to think about.

Unless. . . . Suddenly the events of the past two years crowded into my mind in a momentous sweep. The dreams. The warnings. The fire. My determination to do whatever the Lord wanted—even if it meant leaving my homeland.

No, I had not really committed Peggy's question to the Lord. But I did now. I placed the trip in His hands. It was difficult because I knew with a part of me which I could not understand, that if I left it would not be just for four months. It would be forever.

"Lord, I will say it once again. You know how much I want to stay in my land. After all, I'm 52 years old, and that's not time to start all over again.

"But," I sighed. "But . . . that is not the most important thing is it? All that really matters is staying in Your Presence. Please help me, Lord, never to make a decision that would take me away from Your glory."

14.

Flight

Odd, how after the Lord changed my mind about leaving Pakistan, sudden roadblocks emerged.

One, for instance, that seemed insurmountable was a regulation that citizens of Pakistan are only allowed to take five hundred dollars out of the country. As my dependent, Mahmud could take 250 dollars. How could Mahmud and I possibly live for four months on 750 dollars? This by itself seemed enough to keep us from considering Peggy's suggestion further.

Then a few days later, Peggy invited me to her home for a visit. As we chatted, Dr. Christy Wilson's name came up in the conversation. She knew him too. I was quite concerned about him since I had heard he had been ejected from Afghanistan by the Muslim government which then had destroyed the church he had built in Kabul for foreign nationals.

"Do you have any idea where he is?" I asked.

"Not really," Peggy said.

Just at that moment the phone rang. Peggy went to answer it. When she returned, her eyes were wide, "Do you know who that was?" she said. "It was *Christy Wilson!*"

After we got over our startled, laughing surprise, we began to ask ourselves if this were more than "coincidence."

Dr. Wilson, Peggy said, was just passing through Lahore. He wanted to come out for a visit. Of course I was glad, for it would be good to catch up on news, but I had an intuitive sense that more than casual visiting was going to occur.

We had a marvelous reunion at Peggy's house the next day. I brought Dr. Wilson up-to-date on events in Wah and in my own life. Then Peggy told him about trying to persuade me to come to the United States. He became quite enthusiastic about the idea.

"There are several problems though," Peggy said. "The first is the regulation that Bilquis can take only five hundred dollars out of the country."

"I wonder . . . ," Dr. Wilson said stroking his chin. "I have some friends who might. . . . Perhaps I could send a wire. . . . I know a man in California. . . ."

After a few days Peggy phoned, all excited. "Bilquis," she shouted. "It's all arranged! Dr. Bob Pierce of Samaritan's Purse will sponsor you! Do you think you could be ready to leave in seven days?"

Seven days! Suddenly the enormity of the idea of leaving my homeland swept over me. For I still felt convinced that if I did in fact leave, it would be forever. I understood what Rudyard Kipling meant in his lines:

> God gave all men all earth to love,
> But, since our hearts are small,
> Ordained for each one spot should prove
> Beloved over all . . .

Wah . . . my garden . . . my home . . . my family. . . . Could I seriously contemplate leaving them?

Yes, I could. I could consider nothing else if I were truly convinced that this were God's will. For I knew what would happen if I deliberately disobeyed. His Presence would disappear.

Over the next twenty-four hours another confirmation appeared to come through. Khalid told me at supper that there was only one minor detail left to cover, then all of the real estate problems would be over. "I think you can say quite safely, Mother," Khalid said, "that as of today you have divested yourself of the properties you wanted to sell."

Then suddenly doors slammed. Not by God, so it seemed, but by my country. For still a regulation came in, to the effect that no Pakistani can leave the country unless all of his income taxes have been paid. Mine had been paid, but I needed a statement to that effect. I had to get an Income Tax Clearance Certificate. Only with this could I buy tickets for the United States.

Four of my seven days before departure were gone; only three were left now as my son Khalid and I walked into the government office to get the Clearance Certificate. Khalid and I thought there would be no problems at all, since my papers were in order.

The office was on a busy street in downtown Lahore. However, when I stepped into that building, something struck me as strange. It was far too quiet for the usual bureaucratic office where clerks ran hither and yon and someone always seemed to be arguing with a staff member.

Khalid and I were the only ones in the office except for a bald-headed clerk who sat at the far end of the counter reading a magazine. Stepping up to him, I told him what I wanted.

He looked up only partially and shook his head. "Sorry lady," he said putting his head back down into the magazine again, "there's a strike on."

"A strike?"

"Yes, Madame," he said. "Indefinitely. No one is on duty. There's nothing anyone can do for you."

I stood staring at the man. Then I withdrew a few feet. "Oh Lord," I prayed aloud, but in such a way that only my son could hear me, "have You closed the door? But why did you encourage me so far?"

Then a thought struck me. Had He really closed the door? "All right, Father," I prayed. "If it is Your will that Mahmud and I go to America, You'll have to be the one to arrange for my clearance." A strong sense of confidence filled me and I found myself addressing the clerk.

"Well, *you* seem to be on duty," I said. "Why can't *you* give me my clearance?"

The man glanced up from his magazine with a dour expression. He seemed the type who was always happy to say no.

"I told you, lady, there's a strike on," he grunted.

"Well, then, let me see the officer in charge." One thing I had learned in my government work was that when I wanted something done, I should always go to the highest authority.

The clerk sighed, slapped down his magazine and escorted me to an office nearby. "Wait here," he grunted again, then disappeared into the office. From it I could hear a low murmur of voices, then the man emerged and motioned me in.

Khalid and I found ourselves facing a handsome middle-aged man sitting behind a scarred desk. I explained my need. He leaned back in his chair, twirling a pencil. "I'm sorry Madame . . . Madame . . . what did you say your name was?"

"Bilquis Sheikh."

"Well, I'm very sorry. There's absolutely nothing we can do during this strike. . . ." But suddenly a light of recognition flooded his eyes.

"You aren't the Begum Sheikh who organized the *Simple Living Plan?*"

"I am."

He slammed his fist on the table, then shot up. "Well!" he said. He drew a chair over and asked me to sit down. "I think that was the most wonderful program our country ever had."

I smiled.

Then the officer leaned across his desk in a confidential manner. "Now let's see what we can do for you."

He got me to explain precisely what the problem was and I told him that I was supposed to be in Karachi to catch a plane for the United States in three days. The man's face took on a resolute look. Standing up, he called out to the clerk on the counter. "Tell that new assistant to come in here."

"I have," he said to me in a very low voice, "a temporary stenographer. He is not part of the regular work staff and isn't on strike. He can type up the Certificate. I *myself* will put on the seal. I'm glad to help."

A few minutes later I had the precious Certificate in my hand, fully executed. As I left, I confess, I waved the paper at the surprised little clerk who looked up from his magazine just long enough to see my smile and hear my "God bless you."

As we left the government office building a few minutes later, an astonished Khalid mentioned to me that it had taken only twenty minutes to complete the entire business. "That was less than it would have taken if everyone had been on duty!" he said.

My heart singing, I tried to explain to Khalid that the Lord wants our *companionship*. When we piay, He wants to work *with* us. It was the Moses' Rod Principle. If I had just put the problem in the Lord's hands without stepping out in faith myself, I might never have gotten the Clearance. I had to step out by doing everything I could. I had to ask to see the man in charge. Just as God required Moses to strike the rock with a rod, He asks us, too, to *participate* in the working of miracles.

Khalid seemed a bit taken aback by my enthusiasm but recovered and added with a smile: "Well, I'll say one thing, Mother. I notice that instead of 'thank you' you always say 'God bless you.' And when you say that, it's the most beautiful thing I've ever heard."

Now that all my papers were in order I wondered if I could take a quick trip back to Wah to say goodbye, for by then I was convinced that this trip would be for more than four months. However, when I brought up the subject, Khalid said:

"Didn't you hear about the flood?"

Heavy rains had struck the portion of Pakistan between Lahore and Wah. Many square miles of land were flooded. All traffic was snarled. The government had taken over transportation.

My heart sank. I would not even be allowed to say goodbye. The Lord was asking me to make a clean break, like Lot being told not to look back.

I had planned to leave Lahore on Friday morning, two days off. I would fly to Karachi, the jumping-off place for the United States. Peggy and her son would begin their trip in New Delhi. Their Pan American New York-bound plane would stop at Karachi and Mahmud and I would join them on the plane there. On Thursday morning, however, an unusually strong urge swept over me not to wait. My anxiety centered around Mahmud. Surely grapevine efficiency had taken the news back to Wah that we were not on a simple visit to Lahore but were on our way out of the country. Wasn't it probable that relatives might try to take Mahmud away from my "corrupting" influence! Would I be stopped on some pretext or other? A strong sense of danger spurred me.

No, I wouldn't wait. I would leave that very day. I would go to Karachi, stay with friends, and lie low.

So that afternoon, after a flurry of packing, Mahmud and I said quick farewells to Khalid and his family and hurried to the airport. We flew out of Lahore with a definite sense of relief. We were on our way!

Karachi was, as I remembered it, a rambling desert and seashore town nestled against the Indian Ocean. It was a hodgepodge of the old and new, of gangling camels brushing against Rolls Royces, of buzzing fly-filled bazaars next to smart shops offering the latest Parisian fashions. Perfect. The town was so large we would just be swallowed up in it.

We were staying with friends and I was shopping downtown, preparing for our departure for America the next day. Suddenly a strange oppression came over me. I closed my eyes as I leaned against a wall for support and prayed for my Lord's protection. I was given the strong leading that Mahmud and I were to move to a hotel that night. I tried to shake it off. "This is silly!" I told myself. Then I remembered the story of the Wise Men being warned in a dream to leave early by another route.

Shortly, we were checked into the Air France Hotel at the Karachi Airport. I took Mahmud to the room as quickly as possible, ordered our meals sent up, and together we simply waited. Mahmud seemed restless. "Why do we have to be so secretive, Mum?" he asked.

"I just think we ought to be quiet for a little while, that's all."

That night before the flight, I lay awake in bed wondering. Why was I so apprehensive? There was no real reason for it. Was I letting my nerves take over? Was I overreacting to the threats of the past? The fire? I slept fitfully and only for a few hours. By two o'clock in the morning I was up and dressed, again prodded by a strong sense of urgency. Again I felt ridiculous. It was unlike me. The only way I could explain it was that the hour had come for me to *leave* the hotel and I was being *propelled* by the Lord. I hustled a groggy Mahmud into his clothes, then gathered our bags, placing them by the door for the bellman to pick up.

It was three o'clock in the morning. The flight was at five. Mahmud, still sleepy-eyed, stood with me in front of the hotel waiting for a taxi to take us to the terminal. I looked at the waning moon and wondered, would this be the last time I would see this moon in my own country? An early morning breeze wafted a scent of narcissus, probably from a flower box, and my heart cried out, for I sensed that I would never see my garden again.

Finally the doorman flagged a cab. Mahmud and I climbed in. I prayed as we wove our way through traffic. Even at this early hour the airport avenues were busy. As cars pulled alongside at stoplights I nervously sank back a little deeper into the seat. "We're just being quiet for a little while," I quoted myself, trying to sound as reassuring to my own ears as I had to Mahmud. No, that wasn't the way. What I really needed to do was to pray. "Lord, do take away this nervousness. Nervousness is not founded in You. I cannot trust You and worry at the same time! And yet if this urgency is of You, Lord, there must be a reason and I will obey."

We pulled into the terminal and got out onto a bustling sidewalk where the rumbling thunder of jet engines and the cacophony of hundreds of voices blended in an atmosphere of urgency. My heart caught as I looked up and saw my country's flag, the star and crescent on its green background, snapping in the breeze. I would always respect that flag, my people, and their Muslim faith. A porter hurried our luggage over to the check-in counter where I was grateful to see it disappear into seeming safety.

Just 40 pounds of luggage each. I smiled as I thought of our family trips on other days to the interior when thousands of pounds of luggage were taken for just a few week's stay and my sisters still cried for the clothes that we couldn't take along.

We had an hour to wait before plane time. Keeping Mahmud close to me, I felt it best for us to mix in with the crowd in the terminal so we wouldn't be noticed. But I couldn't shake the sense of impending danger. Again I scolded myself for needless worry. The Lord is in charge, I told myself. He is guiding me out of this situation, and all I need to do is obey.

Then Mahmud asked to go to the restroom. We walked down the hall to the men's room. I waited in the corridor.

Suddenly the loudspeaker called out our flight.

"Pan Am flight for New York City now ready for boarding."

My heart jumped. Where was Mahmud! We must be going!

Finally the men's room door opened. No, it was a turbanned Sikh who stepped out.

I found myself edging to the door. What was I doing! Certainly no woman in a Muslim country would be caught going into a men's room even to look for a nine-year-old missing youngster.

Now they were calling our flight again. "Pan Am flight for New York City is now ready for departure. All passengers should be aboard."

Oh no! My heart cried. I had to do something. I pushed the men's room door back and shouted, "Mahmud!"

A little voice answered, "I'm coming Mum. . . ."

I breathed a deep sigh and fell back limply against the wall. Soon Mahmud came out. "Where were you? What kept you!" I cried.

No matter. I didn't wait for an answer but grabbed the boy's hand and ran. Now we rushed down the long hall to the boarding gate. We found ourselves among the last passengers getting aboard.

"Wow, Mum!" cried Mahmud. "What a ship!"

What a ship indeed. The 747 airliner was huge. We were both excited. I had never seen such a big plane before.

As I was about to step aboard I hesitated for a moment, at this last touch of Pakistan's soil.

But we had to keep moving. Inside the plane, which seemed like an auditorium to me, a stewardess directed us toward our seats. Where was Peggy? What would I do in the States without her?

And then, there she was! Working her way up the aisle toward us. Peggy threw her arms about me.

"Oh precious lady!" she cried. "I was so worried. I couldn't see you in the crowd at the boarding gate!" I explained what had happened and Peggy seemed relieved. She introduced us to her son who was with her. "Too bad we can't sit together," she said. "We just had to take the seats they gave us."

Frankly, it was just as well. My thoughts were not social

at that time. They were on the realization that I was leaving my homeland. I felt sad, certainly, but at the same time *complete*. I couldn't understand it.

Soon Mahmud was being Mahmud. He made friends with a stewardess who took him into the cockpit for a visit. Mahmud came back enthralled. I was pleased. The stewardess asked us to put on our seat belts. I looked out the window to see the first rays of dawn spearing the eastern sky. The engines rumbled and a surge of excitement filled me. Our ship began to lumber down the runway. I looked behind me but could not see Peggy.

But Mahmud's face was there, next to me. And it shone with excitement as the jet engines exploded into thunder at takeoff. I took Mahmud's hand and began to pray.

"What now, Lord? Again I have such a feeling of *completion!* You have brought me out of my homeland, like Abram. Not knowing what comes next, yet complete. Satisfied, because I am with You."

Even embarrassment over my fears and nervousness didn't bother me now. All I knew was that I had obeyed the Lord in every way. And I had to admit that I would never really know what might have happened if I had not followed His every command and moved as I did.

Tiny lights whisked by the windows and suddenly the rumbling of wheels beneath us ceased. We were airborne! In the light of early dawn, I could see the shoreline of Pakistan on the Indian Ocean receding below us.

I held out my hand to Him. He was my only security. My only joy was staying in His Presence. As long as I could stay there I knew that I would be living in the glory.

"Thank You, God," I breathed. "Thank You for letting me travel with You."

Epilogue

1978—Six years have passed since I watched my homeland disappear in the mist. The knowledge that I would not see Pakistan again was prophetic.

I have not been back. The short visit has been extended for many reasons. First of all, my friends have warned that it is best for me and Mahmud—a strapping young man of fifteen and now known as David—not to return. I have been given similar messages from others in authority in my homeland. In 1976 there was a meeting of the Islamic World Congress at which a resolution was passed calling for the withdrawal of all foreign Christian institutions, missionary radio stations and personnel. It's evident that I would not be welcome back in Pakistan now.

Most important, the Lord has made it clear that I remain here; there seems to be a need in America to hear my message. I was first shown this in a vision shortly after arriving in the United States. The Lord was standing in my room. He asked me to speak of His burden for the churches, that there would be a separation of the sheep and the goats and that the judgment would begin at the House of the Lord. I cringed before the task; it was not my place to tell others their shortcomings. I was a visitor in this country and a new Christian. So I asked: "Why me, Lord?"

In answer, His eyes filled with such concern and agony for the churches that I fell to my knees and promised to obey. However, human and weak as I am, I was still hesitant. Was this really from the Lord or was it just me? So I put out a fleece, saying: "If you take me out in spirit, Lord, then nothing in the world will stop me from speaking out." As soon as my head touched the pillow, I was transported in spirit and a great light enveloped me as if I were being anointed for the task.

Clearly and unmistakably, the Lord commanded me to honor and glorify His name and to speak of His mercy and love before churches and groups everywhere.

Then, as if in further confirmation of His direction for me, practically all of the visions that I had back in Pakistan have come to pass, just exactly as I saw them years ahead of time. I have seen in real life some of the American cities and churches so clearly shown earlier in my dreams.

A most startling confirmation that the Lord can speak to us through visions was given to me by Mrs. Harold B. Wold, whose husband is pastor of the Lighthouse Mission Church in Portland, Oregon. She wrote me of a vision she had in America about the same time that the Lord first spoke to me in Pakistan ten years before. "I was walking and praying in my living room," she wrote, "when suddenly the power of God came upon me so strongly that I felt as if my feet weren't touching the floor. In front of me I saw the most beautiful vision. It was a woman of a darker skin, wearing a sari, and somehow I knew she was of nobility. She was facing me and stood for quite a long time, and I knew that when I met her I would recognize her. When you came to our church to speak, I recognized you as the lady in my vision."

Today I live from one moment to the next, waiting to see what the Lord will next do with me and with my time. One thing I know is that I must witness to Him. Another is that I must encourage Americans to appreciate their freedom to worship Christ. And I must pray for my own country. I cannot witness to the people there directly. But when people come to visit me, as my daughters Tooni and Khalida have done, and my son Khalid plans to do, then I can talk freely. Others of my family and friends I will probably never see again. But I pray for them regularly. I pray for all the Muslim people, so close to the living God yet so far, who believe their salvation is a never-ending ordeal of good works. I pray that they will meet the living Christ Who *is* their salvation and that they will meet Him before His second coming.

I think about Nur-jan and Raisham and all the other Christians I left behind. And when I worry about them in their lonely walk, I am assured that He is with them, too. For He promised: *I am not going to leave you alone in the world—I am coming to you* (John 14:18).

The world and its possessions mean little to me now. When I discovered that I would not be returning home, I wrote my family telling them to take my furniture and belongings and give them away or use them as they saw fit. I felt some wrench in this, but there was no other way. Though I must admit that there are a few of my old possessions that I sometimes find myself thinking nostalgically about—the silver dressing case that belonged to my mother and grandmother, and the two small Persian silk rugs in my drawing room. But then . . . it is only momentary, as one does when one recalls a pleasant moment from another day.

I gave Tooni power of attorney, and asked her to put aside funds for the servants' salaries for a year. They had all become like family to me and I wanted to do as much as I could to get them started safely in new jobs.

My gardens and house? I know that the Wah gardens have been taken over by the government, as they are of historical significance. But when I ask about my house where I found the Lord, I get rather vague answers. Perhaps my family and friends are trying to keep me from learning just how bad the house is. What they cannot really understand is that Wah is now behind me. The things of the world have become meaningless to me.

For now my home is in the Lord. My family in Christ is my new family. I am living in the New Jerusalem. It is a place where I have everything and at the same time have nothing. For I have learned painfully, step by step, that when we have nothing at all, that is the moment when the Lord can really begin to work through us. For that is the moment when we begin to live most steadily in His glory.

Bilquis Sheikh

Bilquis Sultana Foundation
P. O. Box 5024
Thousand Oaks, Calif. 91359